STAND UP
AND FIGHT

The Story of Emil Brigg

GEORGE G. HARRAP & CO. LTD

London Toronto Wellington Sydney

First published in Great Britain 1972
by GEORGE G. HARRAP & CO. LTD
182–184 High Holborn, London WC1V 7AX

© *Emil Brigg and Paul Tabori* 1972

ISBN 0 245 50832 5

*Composed in Times type, printed
by The Anchor Press Ltd, and
bound by Wm. Brendon & Son Ltd,
both of Tiptree, Essex*
Made in Great Britain

It was a soft little sound that woke me. For almost thirty years I had slept light as if my ears had learned to respond to the slightest whisper. If you live in hiding and keep company with danger something teaches you to react that way. No matter how tired you are, when you wake you are instantly alert, ready to move or fight.

But there was no danger now. I was in our bedroom in Tel Aviv with my wife, Hanka, breathing gently beside me. I could hear the faint rumble of the traffic and, nearer and louder, the sound of crickets. The scent of night-flowering jasmine came through the window. The luminous hands of my watch showed it was just after three. The sound was repeated and I could tell now that it came from Roni's room.

I slipped out of bed and put on my shirt and trousers. I was very quick and quiet; this too I had been taught by the need to move silently and fast when not only my life but that of so many others depended on it. I could no more break the rules that had to be kept for survival than I could grow wings or an extra nose.

Roni was sitting at his small desk, with a torch in one hand and his ballpoint in the other, writing. He looked up when I stopped behind him and grinned, a little embarrassed.

"It's late," I said, keeping my voice low. "You'll be very tired tomorrow."

"I couldn't sleep, Papa," he explained. "I tried. I really did. There's so much to think about . . ."

I felt that he wanted to talk. In a few hours he was going off to camp; for the first time in his life he would be away from his parents and his sister for several weeks. For the first time, too, they would begin to teach him something about weapons and war; he would start his pre-military training.

Ours is a close-knit family, perhaps because there are so few of us. I brought up my children never to hide anything they feel or think. When they have questions they ask them and we, Hanka and I, answer them to the best of our ability. Now I

5

sensed that Roni was uneasy, that he did not quite know how to put into words whatever was bothering him.

"You want to talk?" I asked.

"Well . . ."

"Come on, then."

We got into the car and drove down Ben Yehuda, turning into Hayarkon Street. I waited for Roni to start, but he was silent as we passed the Dan Hotel and rolled along the seashore with the lights of Jaffa, still undimmed, glittering in the distance.

I stopped the car close to the sea-wall and got out. We sat on the parapet and I lit a cigarette. Roni gave me a disapproving look. He doesn't like my smoking and he keeps on dropping hints, but hasn't had the courage yet for a direct attack.

At last he said, "Papa, did you kill anybody?"

"Yes."

"Many?"

"Quite a few, I suppose."

As I drew on my cigarette I could see my son's face. It was puzzled and tense. I had known that sooner or later I would have to deal with this, but I wasn't properly prepared.

He was silent again and I had to ask, "Why do you want to know?"

"I didn't, not until now. I never really asked you, did I, Papa? I remember you told me once never to hate any single person, whether he be Arab or German. But how can you . . ."

He paused again, then he blurted it out: "I am going away tomorrow and they'll teach me about guns and bombs and hand-grenades. They'll begin to teach me how to kill people. And I am afraid, afraid that I can't do it. I won't be able, when the time comes, to kill someone I do not know, who might be good or evil, kind or cruel, somebody who has never done me any harm. That's why I wanted to ask you . . ."

He stopped and I did not try to hurry him. But when he remained silent I knew that I had to explain.

"You have now started to read books for yourself, Roni," I said. "Not just because you have to or because the teacher tells you. And so, because of the things you are reading and because you are going away tomorrow, I must explain to you the difference between hating and killing. I had to learn it myself. With the Germans it was a question of a nation who set out to annihilate our people. They called it the 'final solution', as if extermi-

6

nation ever solved anything. When a German was given the
order to kill he did it. Well, hardly any refused. And we had no
choice, no chance; they had the guns, the tanks, the planes. We
remained empty-handed to the end, and if we survived it was
by a miracle or blind chance."

"But the Arabs..."

"With them it was different, because we had arms as well as
the Arabs. We had an equal chance. And when I captured
some of them, officers or men, I did not beat them up, I didn't
kill any of them. We were all soldiers; whether justice was on
their side or ours, it made no difference. We fought—but as
soldiers. The Germans invaded country after country, and
when they had destroyed all opposition they began to murder
innocent people, the old, the children and the women. When it
was all over, when they were defeated, I still felt that the guilt
was upon the whole German people. Perhaps the generation
now being born will grow up into quite a decent nation, but I
did not begin to believe even that until quite recently, nor am I
entirely sure of it..."

"And when you killed you felt no guilt?"

"No. Because I killed either not to be killed myself or to
punish those who were murderers."

He looked at his feet and said nothing.

"You understand, Roni, don't you?" I asked him, feeling a
little helpless and wishing he were much smaller so that I could
cuddle him. "You believe me?"

"I believe you, Papa, but I do not understand. Perhaps later
I will. Perhaps."

I drove back to our place and slipped back into bed. But I
could not go to sleep. For the first time in twenty years I
realised that I had to tell my story, so that Roni and the other
Ronis, in Israel and in the world, should understand. I hoped
and prayed that my son and his generation would not have to
kill each other, though peace seemed just as remote that night
as it had done when I was fourteen myself. I had to tell my
story of which not even my wife knew the heart and the
essence.

It is a rather ordinary story and there are men and women
in our street or even in our apartment house who could match
it or top it. Yet I feel that I should tell it for two reasons.
Firstly, to build my own little memorial to the dead, some of
whom fell so close to me and most of whom were slaughtered

7

like cattle; and secondly to make sure that my son and my son's sons should remember this: if you stand up and fight you have a chance of survival. We have had too many martyrs already; our people have shed enough blood; we need not store up a balance to atone for sins or to win the grace of the Lord.

Words came into my mind then, words that expressed it so much better than I ever could. First the words of Uri Zwi Grinberg. I had read his Book of Accusation of Faith, and though I am not as much a lover of poetry as Hanka, I could never forget these lines:

The Jewish tower of corpses is tiered and rises with untold slain-by-and-to-order.

Yet no head has butted away at these heavens! (Head that has turned the edge of a Christian axe or transfixed with a Moslem dagger.) And countless Jews still walk on the globe; old men with clear shining faces whose hands have never shed blood, and comely children with beautiful eyes and bodies as full as the doves. Young men like steel, broad-shouldered and hard of bone, fit for army and navy and fashioning a homeland. Part of these, too, will assuredly serve for cells and tiers in the tower of corpses which my Jewish race will erect in the world.

And all around is a sea of blood, clear to see and ordered by Fate!

The other words were not poetry, but hard and defiant common sense; they were spoken more than half a century ago by Zev Jabotinsky, who taught young Jews the art of shooting straight. His lesson was: "Yiddish blut is nit hefker"—Jewish blood is not cheap. It was for Roni and his generation to prove this once and for all, as I have tried to prove it in a very small and almost childish way.

And finally there were the words of Chaim Nachman Bialik; how right he was, I thought, when he advised God not to waste pity on cowards who did not stand up against the oppressor and tormentor:

Their flesh is wholly sore.
For since they have met pain with resignation
And have made peace with shame,

8

What shall avail Thy consolation?
They are too wretched to evoke Thy scorn.
They are too lost Thy pity to evoke,
So let them go, then, men to sorrow born,
Mournful and slinking, crushed beneath their yoke.

I had refused to bear that yoke; and yet I was alive and had helped a few score, maybe a few hundred, of my people to remain alive. How and why, this is what my story is about.

1

We were to start early that day, Isaac Extermann and I, because it was Friday and we were supposed to be back at the camp for the eve of the Sabbath. Isaac and I were the best cyclists in our whole class and we had our own private races at least once a month. He would cover the distance between Tarnow, our home-town, and Kattowice or Warsaw; I would cycle to Lwow and back. Sometimes I beat him and sometimes he beat me. We were evenly matched. On that Friday, the first day of September 1939, he had turned fifteen and I was a couple of months younger, but we were about the same height and strength.

We were at Piwnicza, deep in the woods near a little stream, a pretty spot. Just before we were to leave, David Schiff, our instructor in the Hanoar Hazioni, the local Zionist group, switched on the small radio in his tent to hear the weather forecast. But instead of the weatherman there was a voice that spoke with a terrible urgency, pausing now and then as if for breath. After listening for a minute or two Mr Schiff stepped into the clearing and called to us to wait. We walked up to his tent, which he had gone back into, and we heard through the crackling and whistling that the Germans had invaded our country at dawn, that there was fighting all along the frontiers, and that all reservists should report at once to their barracks. Then they played the Polish anthem and followed it with a stream of instructions, but by then we were no longer listening. I must confess I felt disappointed about the race Isaac and I had to give up, for Mr Schiff said we should wait until next morning, and then whoever wanted to could stay in Piwnicza and the rest could go home, even though it was the Sabbath, when you were not supposed to travel.

I knew that my family would worry, so I started for home early next morning. Isaac thought he would stay another day or so. I did not see him for almost five years, when I met him by accident in Budapest. From there he walked all the way to Bulgaria and got on a ship which carried illegal immigrants to Palestine. I saw him again four years later, when we were in

11

the same hospital in Bagania. Soon afterwards he fell in our War of Independence.

It took me about five hours to get back to Tarnow and our apartment on Ursulanska Street. I found my parents very worried, for the Germans were reported only about twenty miles away. As I cycled down the main street I could see people queuing up outside the shops buying flour, sugar, and tinned goods, to lay in supplies in case things became short. Many of them had gone through the First World War twenty-five years earlier and had learned by bitter experience how bad things could be.

I found also that I was in the middle of an argument between my father and my mother. They were arguing because Father wanted to leave right away; Mother wanted to stay.

Ours was a typical middle-class Jewish household. Arthur, my father, was the manager of the local pottery works which employed some six hundred people, a large enterprise owned by the Brach family. For two years we lived in a flat on the factory premises and I played in the yard among the fascinating clutter of discarded machinery and broken pottery. The factory produced tiles for stoves and ceramic bricks. Father was the only Jew in the whole place. When he applied for the job he had to provide all the necessary information about himself, his age, his religion, and his experience. He got the job and was shown his office-to-be, which was decorated with a large painting of the Virgin Mary. Next day when he arrived for his work he found that it had disappeared. He sent for the foreman and asked him what had happened to the picture.

"We knew you were an Israelite," the foreman replied, "so we didn't want such a picture to embarrass you."

"Why should a beautiful lady hanging over my head embarrass me?" my father asked. "Bring it back, please." And they did.

Father's great hobby was motor-cycles; he was a racing motor-cyclist who had won many prizes. He even had a uniform like all members of the Cracow Motor-cycle Club, to which he belonged. (Cracow was only about eighteen miles from Tarnow.) It was a very democratic organization; another loyal member was Prince Saugussko, a large landowner. He and my father had become good friends through their devotion to the motor-bike and this soon proved useful to us.

My mother, Paula, was, like all Jewish mothers, a very good

woman. She gave us (my sister, Martha, two years my senior, and myself) every chance to get a decent education, to learn everything useful, to broaden and open our minds. If only time had not been so short! She herself had graduated from the Conservatory of Music in Lwow and with all her household duties never gave up her beloved piano. I hadn't much of an ear for music, but my sister took after Mother and for more than ten years had regular lessons with her. So there was plenty of music in our home, especially as Martha began to collect records and Father always brought some home from his journeys to Cracow and Lwow. Ours was a self-sufficient family bonded together with warmth and understanding; Father called it a "constitutional monarchy" with four autonomous provinces. It was also a Jewish home; though my father did not go every Friday or Saturday to the *shul*, we lit the candles on Friday evenings and the eve of Sabbath meal was as it should be in a Jewish household. Five or six times a year Father *did* go to the synagogue and he had his regular place there. But we weren't Orthodox, though we observed the Jewish traditions, the *Yiddishkeit*, as they say, in our housekeeping and our diet. We were conscious of being Jews—no-one could really escape that in Poland—and we were all members of various Zionist organizations. Father was even president of the Bale Mikcova, the organization of Zionist Experts or Specialists. It was a body of Zionist professional men. From time to time his group sent people to Palestine, trained specialists who were to work there for the foundations of a Jewish National Home. These activities were, if not approved, at least tolerated by the Polish Government; the meetings were held openly and regularly.

So it was only natural that I should spend much of my free time with the Hanoar Hazioni. My school was the Hebrew one called Safa Brura, but apart from two hours of Hebrew and of Talmudic instruction all the other subjects were taught in Polish. School-time was from eight o'clock each morning, except Saturday and Sunday, until a quarter to two in the afternoon. I wasn't very brilliant at things like geography or history, but quite good at mathematics. In the afternoons we had non-compulsory extra lessons for which we could choose our own subjects. I picked photography and carpentry, both of which interested me very much. I became a pretty good photographer by the age of fourteen.

I listened to the argument between my parents, but I couldn't

13

make any useful contribution to it. My sister had gone to spend a few weeks with our paternal grandmother in Delatyn, about forty miles from the town of Stanislawow, in South-eastern Poland. Shortly before I got back from the Hanoar Hazioni camp Father had come home from the pottery. He, like all men of military age, had received orders to leave Tarnow within twenty-four hours and move eastwards, towards the River San. No attempt was made to collect these people, to organize any kind of transport—they were simply given the orders and told to make their way east by whatever means they could. Mother said she would much rather stay and look after our home and then join us later in Delatyn.

Father and Mother talked until eleven o'clock that night. In the end Mother won: *he* agreed that she should stay in Tarnow for a week or so, while *she* promised she would not delay a moment longer than necessary. She said she could always get whatever help she needed from our friends and from people like our former maid Kazha, who had been with us for twelve or thirteen years before she got married to one of the workers at the pottery. She stayed with us almost up to the outbreak of the war, when she became pregnant and had to give up housework. She was, of course, a Gentile—all Jewish households had a servant to do work on the Sabbath—and she loved Mother.

It was with a very heavy heart that my father gave in. The final argument Mother used was that if my sister was on her way back and got to Tarnow after we had left, she would find no-one at home, would not know where we had gone, and would be helpless on her own. It was finally agreed that we would all meet at Grandmother's house in Delatyn.

At four o'clock in the morning Father woke me. I was a little surprised to see him dressed in his motor-cycle club uniform, which was a very handsome one with lots of braid and silver piping. He had to shake me into wakefulness, for I was very tired. I got dressed quickly and packed a few things in my rucksack. Outside the house I found a cart with two horses which Prince Saugussko had given Father. We loaded some food and a few clothes and other things into the cart, with Mother supervising. It was only at the last moment that she turned to me and kissed me and hugged me, saying, "I'll see you soon . . ." She left it that late so that I shouldn't start arguing. I was ashamed to cry, however much I felt like it.

Just before we left an officer passed our house and Father hailed him. He was a major commanding the 16th Infantry Regiment, which was garrisoned in Tarnow, and had been a guest in our house several times.

"Have you any news?" Father asked.

"The Germans have invaded Silesia," he said, "but don't worry, they'll be stopped soon. The English and the French have landed at Gdynia."

"But we were told to leave."

"You must obey your orders, of course," the Major said. "But you'll be back in a few days, I'm sure. Keep in touch!"

It was five o'clock in the morning when we left, Father driving the two horses and I riding my bicycle beside the cart. Soon we found ourselves in the midst of the 16th Infantry Regiment, which was moving east—without the Major. The roads were chock-a-block with soldiers and civilians, with carts, motor-cars, lorries, bikes, all making for the San.

We had travelled only a mile or so when we heard the first explosions behind us. Tarnow was being bombed by the Germans. We were too far away to hear more than the muffled sounds and the terrain hid the town itself from us. It wasn't until weeks later that we had reliable news that it had been a small attack as air-raids went; nobody was killed and only a few people were wounded. But the two-storey house next to my maternal grandmother's home was badly damaged and in danger of collapse. So she moved in with my mother. What happened to the Major who was so certain of Poland's allies landing at Gdynia we never found out—and I never saw Tarnow again.

Before long we had our own danger to meet. We were bound for Kolbusovo-Lazensk, the main crossing over the San. So, it seemed, was a whole Polish army. We offered an ideal target to the Stukas, and soon they came, screaming down upon us, opening up with machine-guns, dropping their bombs.

The whole broad, sluggish snake of humanity seemed to split into scales. The road ran through woods and everybody made for what cover they could find. I saw people pulling a few twigs with leaves over themselves, as if that made them invisible; some crawled into shallow ditches; others, prompted by some crazy logic, began to climb the trees. There was tremendous confusion and in the panic and general mêlée I lost my father for several hours. He couldn't easily get off the road with the

15

cart and horses, while I was pushed off it by some military trucks trying to get past. By the time I got back to the road he had disappeared. And that almost broke my mother's heart.

A mile or two back Father had given a lift to two people from Tarnow he knew—both Gentiles. Before he reached the river crossing one of them said he had had enough of running away—he would go back to Tarnow and take his chances with the Germans. He did manage to get back and went to see my mother. Heaven knows why he took it upon himself, but he told her, "Emil is dead, killed by a German bomb; your husband couldn't even find his body; that's why I came back to Tarnow, to tell you."

At first Mother believed him. But then, somehow, she persuaded herself that it couldn't be true; for the very reason that Father hadn't been able to find me I couldn't be dead. She thanked the Pole and gave him a little money for his pains; he went away and she never saw him again.

I managed to get down to the river crossing and there I suddenly saw Father. It was his uniform of the motor-cycle club that made him easy to recognize as he sat on the box of the cart, looking around to see whether he could spot me in the jostling crowd. I waved and shouted to him and when at last I got to him he was so relieved and glad that he started to call me names and perhaps would have boxed my ears if we hadn't started to move; he had to quiet the horses and coax them down to the approach of the bridge. It took us a couple of hours to get across and we had hardly done so when the planes returned. Their bombs all fell on the western bank of the San and more people were killed in those fifteen or twenty minutes than either before or after during our flight.

It took us twelve days to get to Podhorce, where Prince Saugussko, my father's friend and patron, had an estate and a mansion. Those twelve days were full of noise, clouds of dust, confusion, and danger. We saw thousands of soldiers throwing away their guns; some were making for the west of Poland, trying to get back to their homes; others were so stunned that they just sprawled on the roadside, with no idea what they wanted to or could do. Everywhere there was a vast profusion of abandoned tanks, lorries, scout-cars, and other vehicles that had run out of petrol, for no-one seemed to have thought of building up reserves, providing refuelling centres. Many of them had silly little bits of paper stuck to the windscreen or

16

tailboard, saying: "Don't touch—nothing wrong—only fuel needed!"

More and more civilians were being turned back or forced off the roads. Here Father's uniform proved again a great help. It was pretty dirty and creased and this made it look even more military; the buttons were just like those on an officer's tunic and some soldiers actually saluted him.

We didn't starve, but during the twelve days we were often hungry. In some villages we could buy things, in others they would not accept money, so we had to barter, giving a shirt or a pair of socks for a little bread or eggs. By the fifth or the sixth day we couldn't even do that: every shop was closed and there was nothing to buy from the peasants, as they were hiding whatever they had. It would have become desperate, but the very next day we met the remnants of the 16th Infantry Regiment and there were a couple of officers whom Father knew. They told us we could stay with them and share their rations, which was a great help.

We skirted Lwow, not going into the town as we thought it was likely to be bombed, and continued east. At last we came to Podhorce, where we found another regiment, more or less intact, even well armed. We were given quarters in the little town with a Jewish family. Podhorce was the temporary headquarters of the retreating, disorganized Polish Army. Father went to the Saugussko mansion, where he found some of the municipal council members from Tarnow. They told him that the Russians had invaded Eastern Poland and that resistance in the west had almost ceased, though some forces were still holding out around Gdansk and a place called Westerplatte. The Russians were moving towards Lwow and would arrive at Podhorce before very long. In the meantime soldiers and civilians alike would be issued with passes to cross the Rumanian frontier—we were close to the point where Russia, Poland, and Rumania met—where we would be safe.

But Father would not do that. He thought that if the fighting was over it would be possible to get back to Tarnow, to Mother, and, of course, I wanted nothing better myself. We decided to stay for a day or so at Podhorce before moving west again. As it turned out we would never have reached Tarnow and I think we would have fared even worse in Rumania.

There were about three thousand Polish soldiers in the place, most of them, as I said, still fully equipped, with guns and even some tanks.

Then the Russians arrived. No mighty army, no great force, just a single tank and three Cossacks. They had a loudspeaker on the tank and they ordered everybody to lay down their arms. Three thousand surrendered without a shot, without a murmur. It was then that I began to feel ashamed for the country in which I had been born; it was for the first time that I began to think that I wasn't really part of it, that I did not *belong*. Maybe they couldn't have done very much, maybe even if they had resisted for a short time it would have ended in a massacre, but at least they could have tried. One tank and three horsemen disarming three thousand—it seemed a disgrace.

A single tank crew and three horsemen could not, of course, deal with three thousand surrenders. So the Russians recruited a few dozen Ukrainians, gave them red armbands, and set them to collect and pile up all the arms. It was like letting children into a candy-shop; they helped themselves liberally. The Russian "conquerors" themselves looked far from impressive. Each of the soldiers had a pistol and the tank was equipped with a small machine-gun, besides its six-pounder.

But seeing the Ukrainians swagger as they picked up arms we became afraid.

2

In Tarnow, where I was born and grew up, there were eighteen thousand Jews. About half of them were poor, about 30 per cent well-off, and one-fifth of them rich, at least by our standards. I had never met, in my fourteen years, anybody who hated us. The town council was socialist, and so was the Mayor. Once some Polish right-wing nationalists arrived from Cracow to make trouble. They were so badly beaten up that Red Cross ambulances had to be sent to take them back home. There were only very few Poles in town who felt any sympathy for such people. We knew of them, but they never tried anything violent or even insulting. Now and then there were fights between gangs of boys—say, ten from the Polish high school having a bash at the same number of Jews. I don't know why, but we always got the better of it. My people were not only brave but self-assured; they had a good deal of self-respect and did not humble themselves to anybody, perhaps because they knew that nothing bad could happen to them in Tarnow. Throughout the province of Galicia there were many Jews active in industry, in arts and crafts, rather than in business. In my home-town there were lawyers, physicians, and many professional men and craftsmen. Tarnow had one speciality—confectionary tailoring, a kind of cottage industry. The whole family would work together: the father would cut the patterns, the mother would do the sewing, and the children would add the buttons.

Those years were calm and untroubled, but it was a very fragile, vulnerable existence, as we found out only too quickly. Even during the few hours I spent in Tarnow when I came back from camp and before I went off with Father the surface began to crack. There was much hysterical talk about spies. The rumours were so wild; people were afraid so that they killed first and did not even ask questions afterwards. A Polish lieutenant was shot dead because someone said he was taking photographs of planes flying over the town, though why a spy should do that I've no idea. If someone behaved or looked in a way that gave the impression of his being a foreigner they often decided that he was a German spy or perhaps a Pole of German origin, and he was cut down on the spot. That was a shock for me, however briefly it lasted at that time, because as a child I had never seen such things before. I couldn't even conceive of the idea of treachery. I asked Father, "Why did they kill these people without trial? Without a judge?"

And he said, "That's war, that's how things are in such times."

Now, in Podhorce, with the Ukrainians armed by the Russians and given power, we knew that we might fare like those helpless, innocent people back in Tarnow. The confusion grew bigger and bigger. Those who could crossed into Rumania either just before or shortly after the arrival of the Russians. Prince Saugussko went, and all the nobles and merchants, together with some 80 per cent of the civilians and soldiers. They did not have much time, for the Russians moved fast, and when they reached Brody Zloczow the Polish-Rumanian frontier was closed, though the frontier with Hungary remained open a little longer, until the Russians sealed that off too.

19

Father met another Pole from Tarnow who wanted to get back home. He took our horses and promised to pay Mother for them when he got back. This he did, as we later found out, and in the difficult times that followed he helped her with food and money. He was a good man—one of the few.

Father decided that we must get away from Podhorce before the Ukrainians started trouble. So we asked for a pass to go to Lwow, and then on to Delatyn to stay with my grandmother. The Ukrainian whom he asked first said, "What will you give me for it? If you pay enough you can go." Father sent me away and bargained with the Ukrainian, giving him less than he asked for, but even so it was quite a sum. During those three or four days these Ukrainians made quite a good profit. Of course, our man could have simply taken everything, for the Russians wouldn't have helped us. But we got the two passes, and as the trains were still running, two days later we reached Delatyn. There we found Martha and settled down in Grandmother's house.

Before very long we succeeded in getting a message to Mother in Tarnow, and after a long delay a message came back that she could not leave, that no Jew was allowed to travel, not even a few miles. From time to time there were people who managed to run away from the Germans and cross into Russian-held Poland; they told us that Mother was still alive and well. There was no postal communication between the divided halves of our country even before the Germans and Russians began to fight.

We knew then that we would have to stay in Delatyn for some time, maybe for years. Those two weeks on the road had been exciting, and as I was young I did not mind living rough —I did not even mind the bombs. I didn't have to go to school and Father had treated me like a grown-up, so I had liked it. But now, in Delatyn, we had a little argument. Father wanted me to continue at the *Gymnasium*, the regular high-school, but I wanted to switch to a special technical college. If we had to live under the Russians, I said, it would be best for me to learn a trade. This time I won the argument. I enrolled at the technical school in Stanislawow, some forty miles from the village of Delatyn. I couldn't live in Stanislawow because the Russians wouldn't let Jews or anybody who came from the western part of Poland live in the bigger towns or within sixty miles of the frontier. They were very suspicious of anybody who wasn't born in the territories they now occupied, or perhaps they were suspicious of all Poles, whether Jews or not.

3

It was a new life that began for all of us. Every morning I had to get up at four and walk to the station in Delatyn to take the train to Stanislawow. During the harsh winter of 1939–40 I sometimes had to carry a shovel and dig my way through the snow to the main street from our lane, and often it was sheer ice, so that I slid and slithered for hundreds of yards, falling down and picking myself up from the drifts. In the evening I would take the train back, and after I had eaten I usually fell asleep. There was no time for anything except the journey and the school. I was being trained both as a locksmith and a joiner, working on a lathe. I had to pick up a new language, for half the classes were in Polish and half in Russian. The headmaster was a Russian, not a trained expert or a technician, but just a party man set over the Polish staff, the instructors.

Once a week we had classes in Marxist theory, given by a *politruk*, a party lecturer. There was also a *komsomol*, a Communist youth organization group in the school. While I was there membership was voluntary and out of the twenty-eight boys in my class only five or six joined. Two were Ukrainians, two Jews, and only a single Pole. Now and then the *politruk* would ask reproachfully, "Why are there only five of you in the *komsomol* when in the other class there are already twenty?" We didn't answer him and we avoided discussing the whole business, as we didn't want to get involved. But even those who weren't members had to march with the school on the 1st of May, and when a high-ranking Russian officer, a Marshal or something, came to Stanislawow we were told to put on our best clothes and cheer him. We did as we were told, though some of us shouted all kinds of insults in Polish which were drowned by the screams and the bands playing. We all had to study Russian hard. Speaking wasn't so difficult—there were many similarities with Polish—but writing I found a different matter because of the Cyrillic alphabet which I had never used before. I had learned some Ukrainian when I was quite young, and that was much closer to Russian than Polish. Before too long I could speak fluently enough.

My father tried to get work at once, for neither my sister nor I was working and we needed money badly. Grandmother gave us shelter and she had some reserves of food like all good village housewives, but that wouldn't last for ever. Father could not hope to get a job as a manager or executive; to the Russians he was a *boorzhooy*, a member of the wicked ruling class, an exploiter of the workers. Fortunately he had a second string to his bow. My grandfather Israel used to work for the railways, first as an engine-driver and later as an assistant station-master. He had wanted his son to become a railwayman too, a civil servant, because that meant security and prestige. For a while Father had also worked in the same place as Grandfather, but fairly soon he became interested in business and finally was appointed manager of the Brach Ceramics Works. Now he went back to his first profession and got a job in the railway telegraph and telephone office as a clerk. For a little while he was also an instructor in our technical college, but after a few months they dismissed him because he was a refugee from Western Poland. Like me, he had to travel every day from Delatyn to Stanislawow, though sometimes when he had late duty he slept in the railway workers' hostel.

Though there was peace now in Russian-occupied Poland, life was hard, harder perhaps for us than for the Russians themselves, for we had been used to freedom, to doing as we pleased, to comfort and little luxuries. Nothing was easy, everything quite different from the years of my childhood. Money was practically worthless; the Russians had declared the Polish zloty invalid and had issued very few roubles. We lived mostly by bartering either food or clothes. In Delatyn there were some mineral salt deposits. The Ukrainians who lived there extracted this salt and then travelled sixty, even eighty, miles to barter the salt for wheat. For a pound of salt you could get five or six pounds of wheat or corn. All the time we lived in Delatyn there were no shoes to be had, not even in Stanislawow. If you had a pair you wore them, even if they had holes in them. Sometimes you could have them repaired (if you were lucky), and I had one pair that was mended so often that almost nothing was left of the original shoes; the soles were made of old tyres. It was quite a new craft; all the

22

shoemakers had to re-learn their trade. Boots were made from everything but leather—torn bedspreads, blankets, bits of woollen material. For all food you had to stand in line. When Grandmother woke me at half past three in the morning so that I could catch the train for Stanislawow she gave me breakfast and then went off and queued for bread or potatoes. We got used to spending a fair part of our lives standing in queues.

The Russians did not make things easier by systematically looting the occupied territories. Delatyn was a very poor village, so they couldn't take much, maybe a cow or two or some bedding from the peasant houses. But from Stanislawow they carted away a textile mill, including the concrete foundations. People couldn't understand why all the factories were moved, depriving them of their regular employment. In Delatyn there was a sawmill, but that was left because it worked only for the Russians. The local people could scrounge a bit of discarded timber for firewood; but no-one could obtain any wood for building or repairing houses or for making furniture.

And when there was no machinery, no tools, no individual possessions, to send to Russia, the Russians began to move the only thing that was left—people.

4

On the night of June 29th, ten months after the Germans invaded Poland, both Father and I slept in Stanislawow. Father was on a late shift and could not get back to Grandmother's as the last train left before midnight. I was with a girl until quite late—the sister of one of my classmates. When I left her I went to join my father at the railway workers' hostel; I knew that I could find a place on the veranda at the back where there were a couple of old mattresses. I lay down and went to sleep. But not for long. About 2 A.M. I was awakened by a torch being shone into my face. I heard a voice saying in Ukrainian, "That's one of them!" I blinked; someone yanked me to my feet and said, "Outside! Get into the truck!"

As the torch was switched off I could see several Russian soldiers and a couple of Ukrainian policemen around me. I

23

was still half dazed as I slipped on my shoes and followed them to the front of the hostel where several covered trucks were drawn up. I was told to get into one of them and when I hesitated a little, one of the Ukrainians hit me. I clambered up and almost fell over the legs of my father, who was sitting on a bench along the far side of the truck.

We waited in that truck for more than an hour. A few other sleepy, dazed people were prodded and pushed into the interior —men, women, and children. Some of them we recognized. Most of them were Jews, though several were Polish Gentiles; but all, we found out, had fled from Western Poland to the Russian-held territories. At last the trucks moved off. I stood close to Father and asked him, "Where do you think they're taking us?"

"I don't know, Emil. Perhaps it's just for questioning...."

"But we have passes...."

"Not to live in Stanislawow. And they might say we have broken the law by sleeping here."

The trucks travelled through the quiet town. Two small children began to cry and an old woman, near my father, was moaning and praying softly. At last we stopped. The summer night was already getting lighter. We were outside the marshalling yards. Behind them I recognized the characteristic central dome of the technical college, which was close to the main railway station. Again we waited for over an hour. Then the tarpaulin at the back was opened and someone called to us to get down one by one.

When it was my turn I saw Father, who had jumped down before me, holding out our passes to an NKVD man. He looked at them, shook his head, and said, "No good." (Those were the passes we had bought from the Ukrainian in Podhorce.) Then, before either of us could say anything, he tore them up, dropping the pieces on the cinder path. I thought that it was a pity to have paid so much money for them!

Again we waited until everybody was off the trucks. There must have been four or five hundred people lined up there just outside the gates of the marshalling yards, which stood open. I could just see some goods wagons drawn up, the sort of freight-car which in wartime is usually marked in Central and Eastern Europe 40 MEN OR 8 HORSES.

They counted us again and again, as if they wanted to be sure that they had enough to fill those cars. I wondered whether

24

someone had denounced us, whether Father had any particular enemies in Delatyn or in Stanislawow. It must have been somebody who knew that we would be sleeping in town that night. Or was it just an accident? Or were the Russians rounding up all the Jews, all the people from Western Poland, that night? I worried about Martha, who was in Delatyn and who, I knew, was sleeping that night at the house of a girl-friend of hers. And Grandmother, would they take Grandmother, too? This was not for questioning, as Father thought; they would not bring us to the marshalling yard for that. They were taking us somewhere, someplace far away. I had read about Siberia and everything I had read made me decide it wasn't the place for me.

I began to look around. There were maybe twenty Ukrainian policemen and fifteen or so Russian soldiers in their baggy tunics and topboots. Now someone gave a command and the soldiers moved through the gate. They spread out along the siding on which the freight-train was standing. There couldn't have been more than one to each car. As they moved in, the NKVD man started to count us again. I picked a moment when the nearest Ukrainian wasn't looking in my direction. Then I darted through the open gate. I thought that if I tried to make a dash *away* from the siding they were bound to catch me, or shoot me before I got very far. But they would hardly expect me to try to escape in the direction of the train.

I was right. There was a shout behind me, though I didn't pause to find out who it was and whether it had anything to do with me. Just in front of me, as I got through the gate, was the little platform connecting two freight-cars. I jumped and a few seconds later was behind the train. Another stood on the parallel siding and this time I wriggled under the wheels. Then I ran, taking long strides and leaping over the network of the rails until I reached the low wall at the far end. I pulled myself up, cutting my left palm on something sharp on the top, but I didn't even notice it until later. I dropped into the street, which was deserted, just as the first bell began to ring at the college near by.

I was safe, and during the few minutes it took me to reach my school I had thought of a plan. It was only half formed and I didn't know whether it would work. It depended on the deportation train staying on the siding for a little while longer, half an hour or so. That was probable, because they hadn't even started to load those four or five hundred people, and knowing the Russians I felt sure they would count and re-count. Nor had I seen any trace of an engine when I ran across the rails; perhaps it was still in the shed, getting up steam.

The first classmate I met was called Jan, a Pole, though not a Jew. I grabbed his arm and dragged him into a corner of the corridor. Very quickly I told him what I wanted. He looked at me, incredulous at first, but then he nodded. He was a quick-witted boy, not a particular friend of mine, but he liked pranks and was something of a leader.

"All right," he said. "I'll tell as many as I can find. You go into class—there's still time until the second bell—and . . ."

I remembered that the first class was natural science and our master, an old man, was always late. So I ran, while Jan hurried down the stairs to intercept the boys coming in through the main entrance. I stepped on the dais and shouted for silence. There were about ten boys in the classroom. I told them, quickly and simply, what had happened and what I wanted. Before I had even finished they were rushing for the door.

Most of them lived in Stanislawow, not far from the college, but even those who didn't joined us. Within half an hour we were at the gate of the marshalling yard. We had arrived in groups of three and four, all carrying baskets and parcels, small loaves of bread, or whatever food could be gathered in a hurry. By the time we got there there were other people, grown-ups, jostling around the freight-cars, which still stood on the siding. I called out my father's name and from somewhere half-way down the train heard his answering shout.

Jan was whispering to the boys, looking very serious and important. Half of the wagons were already locked, the heavy sliding doors closed, but some were still open. There was a soldier for every two cars, rifle at the ready, but the Ukrainian auxiliary policemen had disappeared. Jan and his group con-verged on one of the open doors and I took the rest of my class-mates to the one from which I heard Father calling. He was standing near the door, shaking his head. He was probably angry with me for coming back when I had already got away. There was no time for explanations. The soldier guarding this particular car was shouting at us to go away, but the boys pressed closer, raising their arms with the little packages, offering them to the people nearest to the open door. I got in front and called to Father in Polish to wait a little and then

jump when I shouted. He stopped shaking his head. The
soldier was struggling with his rifle; the sling had caught in one
of his buttons. The boys were now surrounding him so that he
could barely move and couldn't see what was going on outside
the circle. I shouted to Father and he jumped—so did three
other men. The guard was still trying to get his rifle free. The
boys were talking to him, patting his back, one offering him
some tobacco, another fingering the cloth of his tunic. I took
Father's arm and pushed him forward. The other three men
had turned in a different direction. We crawled under the train.
The next siding was now empty and we ran, leaving the confused voices behind. There was a shot, then another—then
silence. By then we were over the wall and Father began to
laugh. Then he noticed my hand, which was still bleeding a
little, and he said, "You should be more careful. Put your
handkerchief around it. Have you got a clean one? Here, let
me do it for you. . . ."

I let him do it because I knew that he needed to show that
he was in charge, that he was the head of the family. And I
laughed, too.

5

We did not stay in Stanislawow, but returned to Delatyn at
once. We did not go to my grandmother's house lest they
should be looking for us, but stayed at a neighbour's. There we
discovered that the same night a hundred and fifty people had
been rounded up in Delatyn too, refugees from Western Poland
like ourselves, most of them Jews. Martha had escaped because
she was staying with her girl-friend outside the village. And
Grandmother they did not take, because she had lived there
all her life. Later we found out that that night the Russians did
the same thing in Lwow and in many other places where the
refugees had settled. They were all shipped to Siberia, the place
I had no liking to go to. Very few, if any, ever came back,
though later some of the Poles were allowed to join the Anders
army.

After two days Grandmother ventured out and went to the
house of a Ukrainian whom she had known for some years and

whose brother had worked for my late grandfather. She knew how to bargain and he said he would act as a go-between with the Russian in charge of passes at the village police station. It cost a great deal of money and we also had to give the Ukrainian a bicycle, but after ten days spent in hiding we got our papers. Our birthplace was given as Delatyn, which meant that we were no longer classified as refugees, which was why it cost so much money. It gave us a little more security.

I went back to the college in Stanislawow. The boys were glad to see me and Jan said that he and his group had managed to get half a dozen people off the deportation train, though two of them were later recaptured. The masters asked no questions and for a whole year, until my graduation, I was left in peace.

It was different with Father. Whoever had denounced us was working in the same office at the railway, so he was suspect and could not go back to his old job. So he moved to Kolomyja, where we had some distant relatives with whom he could stay and where he became foreman in a workshop that manufactured and repaired water-pumps. Thus we were, like so many families, scattered and divided: Mother, though she made several attempts to get an exit permit to join us, still in Tarnow; Father in Kolomyja; Grandmother and Martha in Delatyn; and I in Stanislawow, because with the new forged pass I did not have to commute every day.

As the months passed and the harsh winter of 1940–1 was followed by a late and reluctant spring, I became more and more unhappy at my college. Not because of the work: I loved to do things with my hands, I loved to handle tools and make little useful objects. But there was an atmosphere of suspicion and distrust. We knew nothing about what went on in the world outside the small circle of our lives. The radio just broadcast propaganda and few people listened to it except maybe for the weather forecast and the sports results. No-one spoke about politics, because everybody was afraid. If someone ever said something political, by accident or because he was carried away, chances were that he would be denounced, arrested the next day and kept in the NKVD prison for two or three days. If he was weak or easily frightened he would confess, admit that he said this or that, and then he was sent to Siberia without a trial, convicted as a "spy" or "guilty of conducting anti-Communist propaganda". After this had happened once or twice, and a student and a master disappeared, no-one opened his mouth. Two boys, among them Jan, were expelled because they refused to attend some parade or demonstration. It was something to do with the *komsomol*, and even though neither of them was a member, they were kicked out and did not get their diploma. The only job they could get was digging ditches or as stevedores.

Some of us began to think of running away, going to Hungary, which was not so far away and where the frontier was not so strictly guarded. From there, we were told, one could get to Palestine. That was only a dream, of course, something to talk about when we were particularly unhappy. Even then we would not talk about it at the college or in our homes. We would take a walk far into the countryside, along an empty highway where we could not be overheard. We were afraid of our non-Jewish classmates, and even of some of our own faith who might betray us.

We could not imagine how the rest of the world was faring. We had heard that France had capitulated, but knew nothing about the Battle of Britain. I only heard about it almost five years later. In the whole of Delatyn there were only five radios and the Russians took great care that no-one listened to the foreign stations. Even if we had had the chance to do so, they threatened such penalties that it would have been foolhardy. The newspapers carried no foreign items. They wrote about the wonderful progress in the Ukraine, in Russia proper, but nothing about the events in the world outside the Soviet Union. I didn't even know most of the time what was going on in German-occupied Poland, until I went to Lwow, where I met some people who had run away from the other side and they told me a few things. But that was only in the spring of 1941, when we had a week's holiday at the college. I had heard that some friends of mine from Tarnow had crossed over and were in Lwow; I met them at the home of a former classmate of mine who was living there. They told me how the Jews fared under the Germans, and said, "Never go back to German-occupied territory if you are a Jew." Some Poles, Gentiles, did travel west, running away from the Russians, thinking that it might be better under the Germans. One always hopes that another part of Hell might be less hot, the torments less. But I was told in Lwow, "Don't. No Jew must risk putting himself under German terror." The death-camps had not yet been established, but the Jews were all rounded up for forced labour. There were, of course, some places where they had started to kill the Jews, but they hadn't got going properly yet, they hadn't the complete organization for what they later called the "final solution". So I came back to Stanislawow, and later went to Kolomyja to tell Father what I had heard and that we must try to get Mother away from Tarnow before it was too late.

6

Early in June I graduated from the technical college in Stanislawow. I had worked hard, and I gave myself a couple of weeks' holiday before starting work. I was almost seventeen, strong, healthy in spite of the frugal fare on which we lived, and I was quite popular with the girls. I did not bother to think about the future. I was content with whatever enjoyment our simple and arduous life offered, which wasn't much, but it was enough.

Then, near the end of the third week of June, we began to notice that something was up. The Russians were bustling to and fro, lorries full of soldiers drove down the streets, equipment was moved; there did not appear to be any general purpose to all this, but still it was unusual. Somebody said that we might be attacked, but no-one knew whether such an attack would come from German-occupied Poland or from Hungary, or even from Rumania. And we weren't even sure who the attackers might be.

I was in Delatyn, staying with my grandmother and Martha. The village had a small Russian garrison and on June 21st it moved out without a word, without any reason being given to the people. The Russian administrators also left, and suddenly we were without any local government, without any authority.

For three days and three nights this state of affairs continued; we were suspended, like Mohammed's coffin, hovering between heaven and earth. However, within a few hours of the Russian departure we got a taste of what was in store for us.

Like wolves invading a deserted farmstead, the Ukrainians moved into the village. There were a few isolated houses outside the main settlement, all of them occupied by Jew families. Those they attacked first. They looted them, cleani out everything that could be moved, even the large cookin̫ pots; then they hanged them, men, women, and children, outside their homes. I had slipped out to find out what was happening and watched it all from a near-by thicket. Then I ran back to Grandmother's. We barricaded ourselves hastily in her house, and another Jewish family that lived opposite came to join us. Our house had a strong stone wall on the ground floor with a wooden superstructure and this gave some protection against bullets, at least so we thought. And apart from me there were four other men, so we hoped we could defend ourselves, even though we had no arms except a few kitchen knives and a spade or two. I don't suppose we could have done much, though. But we were at least determined not to be slaughtered like cattle.

That night the Ukrainians set fire to the house opposite. We watched it burn down through the cracks of the shutters; first they moved every piece of furniture, every article of clothing, from it. There were some fights over the spoils (I remember that two Ukrainian women came to blows over a small, rather shabby piece of fox fur), and they must have also looted the cellar of the village inn, kept by a Jew, for most of them were rolling drunk.

They were like animals let out of cages unexpectedly. Of course, most Ukrainians hated all Jews, but those of Delatyn also had accounts to settle, in more than one sense of the word. One of the families they massacred kept a grocer's and bakery. Many of the Ukrainians owed them money, and they hated them just because the Jews gave them credit. These were the Zauderers, and all seven members of the family, including the old, blind grandfather and a small girl of three, were killed. Another Jewish family was living opposite the saw-mill, and all nine of them were driven to perish in the flames of their own home.

All night and for the next three days and nights we waited in our house, expecting any moment that it would be our turn. We stood guard at the front windows, four hours each, watching the street. But they never came. I still don't know why. Perhaps because of the Ukrainian whom Grandmother had bribed to get us our forged passes; perhaps they had just had enough of looting and killing. There were about two thousand five hundred Jews in and around Delatyn. Some hundred and twenty were killed during those four days of terror. So we weren't the only ones who had a lucky escape.

Then, in the afternoon of the fourth day, the soldiers arrived. At first we thought they were Germans, but we soon realized that they spoke a language we couldn't understand. Before long we found out that they were Hungarians.

When the troops arrived the Ukrainians who had come in from the villages and farms around Delatyn to do the looting and killing ran away. We soon noticed that the Hungarians had no intention of harming us. They organized a new local police with some Polish and Ukrainian volunteers, not those who had taken part in the four days' frenzy, but others. As they say, a new king always finds courtiers if he wants them. But it seemed that all the Hungarians wanted was to establish order; they told us to open up the shops and get back to normal life.

After a few days we noticed that not all Hungarian troops were the same. Quite a few were unarmed, their uniforms were without any marks, except yellow stars. We addressed them in German and in Yiddish and quite a few answered. They were Jews who had been drafted into labour camps in Hungary and were brought straight to Poland from these camps to work as auxiliaries—a kind of pioneer corps. They seemed to be quite well treated by their gentile officers and N.C.O.s, and above all they had food. Not very large quantities, but still enough and to spare. They gave us some when they found out how short we were and we made friends with quite a few of them. Later new food supplies arrived and the Hungarian *munkaszolgálatos* (labour service) troops shared their rations with us. The railway between Delatyn and Hungary through Vorochta Vorchinka on the Polish and Körösmezö on the Hungarian side was repaired and reopened. For those three months, from late June till late September 1941, while the Hungarians were in occupation, we led a normal life—well, as normal as it was possible in wartime.

Though Father had come to visit us in Delatyn several times, he did not want to stay. He was now working in the vehicle repair shop in Kolomyja, which served the District Commandant's office, the military police, and the Gestapo. This was run by three other Jews, the Feigenbaum brothers, supervised by a German sergeant.

One day in August I went to see him. When I got there the

Germans, two privates and an N.C.O., were beating him. He did not say anything, just tried to protect his face and head from the blows. I stood outside the door and was almost blinded by rage and tears. No-one had ever hurt my father in my presence; I couldn't imagine why anybody should want to do this to him. I bent down to pick up a stone and was about to throw myself at them. But at that moment they stopped. Father was bruised and swayed on his feet; he was bleeding a little. The Germans then grabbed his arms and took him away.

I wanted to follow him, but one of the Feigenbaum brothers pulled me back.

"It will be all right," he said. "Don't go after him or you'll get in trouble. But if you like you can wait."

I waited and in a couple of hours Father came back. He had washed his face and did not look too bad. It was only then that he noticed me for the first time. He tried to smile, and after a while he even succeeded.

"It's all right, Emil," he said. "They put me in charge of the workshop. I am the technical manager now."

"But why were they . . ." I couldn't quite bring myself to say "beating you".

"They wanted me to repair a small dynamo, but the most important part was missing and they couldn't give me a spare. I tried to explain when they came for it, but they wouldn't let me. They took me to the Gestapo, and there I found one of the officers for whom I had rebuilt his whole car-engine. I had worked three whole nights to get it ready. He recognized me and let me explain; he bawled out the soldiers and said that from now on I was to be in charge and was to report to him if there was any trouble . . ."

"Yes, but if you hadn't found that officer there . . ."

"What kind of foolish talk is that, Emil? I found him, and that's all that matters."

I realized then what the Germans were like: you could not tell what would happen from one day to the next, which of them would turn into a wild beast and which would listen to reason. I thought it would be best if the family were together in the same place; at least we could try to help one another. I could work with Father and Martha could find some job in the bigger town. I told Father and he said all right, he would get some place for all of us to live in.

Next day I went back to Delatyn and fetched my sister.

Travel wasn't easy, because we couldn't use the railways, but we used to get a lift on some Hungarian army lorry or find a Ukrainian driver with a cart to whom we would give a few cigarettes for a lift. Though it was only about twenty-five miles from Kolomyja to Delatyn, sometimes it took two or three days to cover the distance.

When I safely delivered my sister into Father's care I worked for a week at his workshop to make a little money before I went off to fetch Grandmother. It was late September, but still warm and dry weather. A cart took me half the way to Delatyn and put me down at the crossroads. I decided to spend the night at Nadvornaja, a village only three miles from the crossroads where my friend Jossek Wundermann and his family lived.

I got there in less than an hour, and Jossek was happy to see me. So was his family. They gave me a good supper, and then we went to bed. I was to start out for Delatyn about eight o'clock, but about five Jossek's father came into the room I shared with his son. He was white as a sheet and he was clasping and unclasping his fingers, cracking his knuckles.

"The Germans," he said. "They're in the next street, rounding up all our people. They'll be here any moment. . . ."

I quickly put on my clothes and ran to the back of the house. But it was too late. There were the SS men with their death's-head caps and a group of Gestapo officers. From every house they were driving the people into the street, shouting, screaming at them. Some had whips which they cracked, and now and then let the twisted, plaited leather thongs descend on the backs and buttocks of the old ones and the children. There was much wailing and confusion. I looked around, but I saw no way to escape, for there were too many, and now I noticed that soldiers with automatic rifles stood on the top of lorries, watching. One of them fired a couple of rounds when a small girl broke loose and tried to run back into the house. They drove us, with whips and abuse, into the market-place, which was completely ringed with armed Ukrainians and SS men. Jossek and I stood near the fountain and clambered up. From all the streets groups of Jews were being herded into the square, men, women, and children, old and young. More and more came, and soon the place was black with them. Some were half-naked and shivered in the keen morning air; a few carried bundles as if they were prepared for a journey.

We stayed in the market-place until noon, with the Ukrainians and the SS men all around us, chatting, laughing, now and then pointing with their riding-crops at one or the other person, a girl or an old man, as if they were inspecting cattle in a pen. Then a fleet of lorries arrived and they started to load the people onto them. Now there was a great deal of shouting, and when some did not move fast enough or stumbled the guards beat them and kicked them. Gradually the square emptied and the lorries were full; people stood up in them, crowded together, barely able to move, arms, legs, and bodies pressed against one another, so that you could hardly tell where one person ended and the next began.

I kept close to Jossek and whispered to him to try to get on the last lorry. "No need to be pushy!" I said. He didn't ask me why, and if he had I couldn't have really told him. I just had a feeling that it would be better. And we *did* manage to get into the very last group. It was now about half-past one in the afternoon, and the lorries moved slowly out of the square, along the main street of Nadvornaja, which wasn't very long. It was deserted, though here and there you could see a little movement behind the curtained windows where people were watching. Then we left the village behind and took the road that led to the forest called Bukovinka. It was a large, ancient forest without much undergrowth, but with towering pines and oaks. The pines were green, but the other trees had put on their autumn colours and some of the leaves were blood-red or dark yellow.

After driving down the highway for about half an hour the lorries turned off along a broad forest path which was deeply rutted. They swayed and slipped and we were squeezed even closer against each other. Then they suddenly stopped. I was near the front of the lorry and taller than most, so I could see the clearing at the edge of which we had halted.

At the near end there was a long trestle-table with some SS officers and guards sitting or standing behind it, as if they were having some sort of a picnic. But instead of food and drink, the table was covered with clothes, all kinds of clothes, trousers, jackets, skirts, shifts, children's shorts, and petticoats. And we heard the voices, roaring at us to undress, to put our clothes in one heap and our documents in another.

In the centre of the clearing there were two large shallow pits, about fifteen or twenty yards across. One of them was already full to the brim with naked corpses. Their colour stood

35

out clearly from the brown earth and the carpet of fallen leaves that edged the mass grave. There was very little blood. But as we clambered from the last lorry, Jossek jumping to the ground just before me, I saw how a group of ten people was lined up on the edge of the second hole, men, women, and children, totally naked. Two or three were shivering, but the others stood still. Then the SS men raised their automatic guns, there was a short burst and the bodies fell. Some just slid to their knees slowly and then toppled over; others dived forward as if they were plunging into a river or lake. Before they had completely disappeared, another ten were lined up. I stared, I couldn't take my eyes off them, until an SS man kicked me and screamed, "Go on, pig, undress!"

I stripped completely. I did not feel anything, no fear, no anger, nothing. I didn't think of praying or of running away. Maybe that's how rabbits behave when a stoat corners them. There were only about fifty of us left when one of the two Gestapo officers who sat behind the centre part of the trestle-table and who had been writing something in an exercise book looked up. (Later, much later, I found out that he was in command of the whole operation, a man called Gregor Schipper. He was a very handsome man with a trim moustache and a faint duelling scar, a *Schmiss*, on his left cheek.)

He said to the officer next to him, "That's the total for today, the full quota."

And the other man nodded, raising his voice, "Listen, Jews. Anybody who has gold or money or jewellery, he can go!"

Next to me a little fat man who had been clutching a small package in his left hand slithered forward to the table, dropped the package, then turned, running as hard as he could, his fat buttocks waggling in a ludicrous manner. I thought, Now! They are going to shoot him down! But the SS men only laughed and nobody fired. Nor did they kill the next one, an old man who was so hairy that he looked like a man-shaped rug. They *did* hit him a few times, probably because he didn't have enough valuables; but he too was allowed to disappear among the trees.

I was the third in the line. All I had were a few occupation marks, the money the Germans issued, and the gold watch which my father had given me for my *barmitzvah*. I put it on the table.

"You call *that* something?" I heard a voice behind me

36

screaming, and then I felt a terrible blow on the side of my head. It must have been a rifle-butt. And yet I turned and began to run like the others. I could feel the pine-needles and the cold little stones under my naked feet. And then the ground seemed to rise and I fell, and it became quite dark and very peaceful.

7

When I woke it was still dark, even darker than before. I could see nothing. For a moment I thought I was dead. Then—and this frightened me even more—that I was alive but in some prison. I stretched out my arms and felt all around me, but there was nothing, no walls, only the air. Maybe, I thought, I had gone blind, and I was terrified. I touched my face and found it was swollen and painful and my eyelids were stuck down with dried, coagulated blood. Gently and slowly I scraped and rubbed at them until I could open my eyes.

I was still in the Bukovinka forest. Night had fallen, but moonlight came through the trees in broad shafts and I could see quite well. I was very cold, and when I tried to get to my feet I fell back and was sick, retching for a long, painful time until I was completely exhausted. I tried again and managed to rise shakily.

The clearing was empty now: nothing and nobody moved. The trestle-table was gone. But in the middle there were the two large pits. Only they were quite full, full to the brim. The Germans did not think it worth the trouble even to cover them with a thin layer of earth.

I began to search for Jossek, but could not find any trace of him, nor of anybody else I knew. Perhaps he had escaped (though I never saw him again); perhaps he was in that second hole which had still been half empty when we had first arrived in the clearing.

Here and there I came upon bodies that had fallen close to the edge of the open space. Most of them were lying on their faces—they had been shot in the back. So perhaps after they had let the first few go the SS started a little target practice on the rest. Or some may have survived the automatic weapons on the edge of the mass grave and tried to crawl or run away and were stopped short. . . .

Some of the corpses were still half dressed. I hesitated a long time before I could bring myself to remove the trousers from a tall, thin man who was about my size. But I was naked and it was getting colder and colder in the forest. And if I wanted to get back to Delatyn (that was the only plan I could think of) I had to have a pair of trousers at least. I put them on, and then, a little emboldened, I stripped the shirt off another body, that of a young boy. Shoes I could not find anywhere. I suppose they were too precious for the Ukrainians to leave uncollected.

When I had finished my foraging I felt weak and dizzy, so I sat down as far as I could from the clearing and those two holes with their silent contents. I dozed off, though I did not dare go to sleep; somehow in my confused state I thought that the Germans might come back. But they didn't. The moonlight faded, there was a grey mist creeping between the trees, and then gradually it became lighter. It was still not full daylight when I started off, barefoot and aching in every limb. My face was still swollen and I couldn't clear off the caked blood, as I found no water.

It was almost ten miles to Delatyn and I did not get there until the evening. I had to rest again and again because I was so weak, but after each pause I forced myself to go on. Also, I did not want to arrive in the village in broad daylight and call attention to myself.

At last I reached my grandmother's house through the back-yard. I scratched softly at her window. After a while it opened. "It's me," I whispered, "Emil."

She opened the back door with a lamp in her hand. She almost dropped it as her eyes opened wide, and her mouth too, as if she were about to scream.

"For the love of God, what's happened to you?" she asked.

I pushed past her and closed the door. There was a little mirror on the chest of drawers and for the first time I could see myself. I *did* look awful, my lips cracked, my face swollen, one eye almost closed, and an ugly bruise along my left temple.

I asked for a drink and she brought me some milk. Then she asked me again, and I told her, though I found it wasn't easy. She said nothing, but just kept looking at me as if she couldn't believe her eyes. Then she got up and put on her black shawl. "Come," she said, "I'll take you to Dr Bernstein."

We walked down the back alleys to the doctor's house a couple of streets away. He washed off the blood and found that my skin was still open in one place. He bandaged me and gave me a pill for the pain.

"Whom did you fight?" he asked when he had finished.

"He has such a story," Grandmother said. "You never heard the like of it, Doctor."

I told him then, a little more coherently and fully. He looked at Grandmother and said to her, "Why don't you go home, Mrs Brigg? I'll talk with Emil a little while."

Grandmother left and the doctor made me sit opposite him.

"Now, Emil," he said, "you have been to the cemetery here in Delatyn?"

"Yes, I have." I didn't know what he was after.

"How many people would you say are buried there?"

"Two or three hundred," I said. "Maybe more."

He shook his head. "And you want me to believe that in two shallow holes some twenty yards across the Germans could bury a thousand or twelve hundred people? Just try to figure it out, it's impossible."

I told him that I didn't have to figure it out. There were some twenty or twenty-five lorries, with at least fifty people on each. I knew what I had seen, and if he didn't believe me I couldn't help that.

He was still sceptical and I felt too tired to argue. So I went away. Later he sent for Grandmother and told her that I must be still suffering from shock, that I couldn't possibly know what I was talking about. She was to keep me at home and let me rest. I would get over it.

So I sat at home in the darkened back room, but I did not rest and I did not get over it. The swelling went down, the bruises faded, though I still had the scar. And when I looked into the mirror I noticed that my hair was still white with dust. I washed it, and then I realized it wasn't dust. There were patches of white. At seventeen I had gone grey during the night in Bukovinka forest.

But there was something else that filled my hours during the next ten days while I waited for my wounds to heal. For the first time in my life I began to think about life and death, about cowardice and courage, about people. Until then I was only concerned with tangible things, with riding my bike, with food and drink, with girls, and with the feel of the tools I was using.

39

Again and again, like a film in a projector that was stuck, I saw the people being lined up on the edge of the mass grave, the SS men lifting their weapons, the shots, the slow or sudden collapse of the naked bodies. I tried to drive these images away but they came back. I thought that the lucky chance of survival, that I was one of the few who weren't killed, put me under an obligation. And I swore that I would fight as long as I had breath in my body, that I would never give in, however desperate things looked, that I would survive. It wasn't a very logical or sensible pledge—I couldn't even guess what would happen tomorrow or the next week—but I made this pact with myself. I suppose I grew up during those lonely days; in a way I became older than my grandmother and my father.

Two weeks after the massacre in Bukovinka forest, about the end of September 1941, some German civilians arrived in Delatyn. Their task was to rebuild the bridge over the Przesmyk river which the Russians had blown up. It was an essential link in the railway network, for the line to Czernowitz in Rumania and to the Hungarian frontier-station Körösmezö both passed through Delatyn. The civilians belonged to the Todt organization, and they opened a labour office in the village.

Grandmother came home one day and told me about it; she also said that the Germans were going from house to house, rounding up all able-bodied men, from fifteen to sixty-five. You could, however, volunteer, and that would mean better treatment. Our food-supplies were very low and I decided that I would volunteer; in any case, I was getting tired of skulking in that airless back room and letting Grandmother do all the work.

The repair gang was a motley one. There were some German Jews drafted for the labour service; there were some Ukrainians and Poles, many of them also Jews. The Polish Jews were given a plate of soup for wages, and we worked from seven in the morning until six in the evening. The Poles and the Ukrainians were paid a few occupation marks in addition.

We Jews were also given the toughest job. We had to drag immense wooden spars from the rafts which had been floated down the River Przesmyk up through a deep ravine to the spot where the new bridge was being built. Each of them was about sixty feet long and four or five feet thick. Six ropes were attached to them and there were four or five people pulling on each rope. The floor of the ravine was rocky and uneven and in places very steep. At intervals a German overseer stood along the path we had to follow, watching and marking the rhythm of our movements with shouts. If anybody slackened off or stumbled he was beaten with whips and sticks until he collapsed. There was no consideration shown for the old or the weak, and every day there were one or two deaths. We worked seven days a week, without a break.

After seven or eight days all the spars which were to be used as piles of the bridge had been dragged up the ravine and manœuvred into position. Now they were to be connected and strengthened with iron brackets and traverses. I was attached to a group working with heavy hammers, fastening these iron parts to the wooden structure. Most of the people in these groups were Ukrainians, except for three Jews, as the rest didn't know how to handle the heavy hammers. Because this was particularly hard and dangerous work (we were perched over the fast and treacherous river and sometimes had to continue in driving rain and high winds) we were given an extra plate of soup and half a pound of bread.

After we had finished this job the wooden spars and crossbeams had to be treated with tar. This was filthy work, and all done by Jews. We asked for a chance to clean up after each day and the Germans said, sure, there were some open-air pools where we could bathe. They did not tell us that the water was mixed with quicklime. After three days of such "baths" our bodies were covered with sores. So we gave up trying to clean off the tar; we began to look like black men or strange freaks, for all kinds of dirt would stick to the tar. It wasn't until Grandmother brought home some surgical spirit from Dr Bernstein that I managed to get rid of this crust, and it took over a month before my sores were healed. Others were not so lucky and several died of the infection.

8

One evening as I walked home from the river I noticed two Gestapo men leading ferocious-looking Alsatians on steel leashes.

I tracked them for a while until they disappeared into the

former village hall. I ran home and told our neighbours that something evil was brewing, and pleaded with them to hide and to pass on the warning. Before long the grapevine had spread the news all over Delatyn. We had no cellar or ice-pit, so I hid Grandmother in the house of the Ukrainian who had got us the forged papers and who was still on friendly terms with us. I hid in the attic, which was small and low and not easily discovered.

Nothing happened that night and in the morning the men, as usual, went off to work, though the women and children remained in hiding. During our short break at ten o'clock I slipped away from the river and back to the village.

In the meantime the Jews who had been in hiding gradually emerged from their various, pitiful places of safety. They thought that as the night had been peaceful and no-one had harmed them in the morning, nothing would happen now. They even greeted the German SS men and soldiers politely and humbly and received a tolerant if not particularly warm *"Heil Hitler!"* in exchange.

Reassured, I went back to the bridge, as I did not want to be missed. But less than an hour later a small boy clambered down the steep embankment where we were working, and soon we knew the worst: all the Jews in Delatyn were being assembled in the market-place. There was nothing we could do, for we were under armed guard and as soon as any of us stopped there were blows and screams of abuse. Around noon I saw some Gestapo men approaching the river. As soon as I caught sight of them I threw down my tools and began to run along the river. They saw me and started to fire at me, but I zigzagged across the smooth, sandy bank, then plunged into the water, swimming downstream, keeping under water as long as I could. Still they kept on shooting, but I wasn't a very clear target and wasn't hit. A mile or so downstream I waded to the shore and, describing a large circle, made my way back towards Delatyn.

I kept as much under cover as I could, in the backyards and among the bushes. Already at the outskirts of the village I could see how people were being driven along by Germans and Ukrainians. Here and there when someone could not move fast enough or stumbled, he was gunned down. I did not enter the village proper, but turned away and reached the forest across the fields and back lanes. Here I wandered round on the narrow

42

paths, for I was afraid to cross the highways or the main tracks, which were bound to be guarded, until late at night, and then I settled down under a pile of dry leaves. I dozed off and woke again, afraid to go to sleep. In the morning I heard several volleys, then a pause, then again a lot of shots close together. Now came a long period of silence, broken by several single shots. I cautiously followed the direction of the shots, and then, from a perch in a tall and still thickly foliated tree, I watched some Ukrainians walk towards the highway, their arms full of clothes, boots, and other loot. I remembered the Bukovinka forest, of course, and guessed what must have happened. I waited for long hours, pressed close to the trunk of the tree, then I climbed down. Not far away I found another mass grave heaped with corpses left uncovered.

I felt scared and lonely. I made my way to the railway tracks and followed them most of the way, hiding whenever I heard a train approaching or when I got near a signal-box or a station. The twenty-five miles to Kolomyja took me two and a half days. I had a little bread in my pocket and I stole potatoes from the fields and a few cobs of corn which I roasted in some lonely spot—a hollow or a ruined hut. The nights were getting cold and I only had the clothes I wore at work, dirty and ragged. The third evening I got to Kolomyja and went to my father's lodgings. He and my sister and our cousin Janek Seibald were having supper. They were startled to see me in such a state and I could hardly speak. They fed me, and Father gave me a little vodka because my teeth were chattering. Then I told them what I had seen in Delatyn and in the forest.

Father immediately asked about Grandmother and I told him that I had hidden her in the house of the friendly Ukrainian. But that did not satisfy him and next morning he sent me back to fetch her. She would be safer with us in Kolomyja, he thought, where his work for the District Commandant and the Gestapo was some sort of protection. I did not argue, for to tell the truth my conscience was bothering me: I should have gone into Delatyn, I told myself, and made sure that Grandmother was all right instead of running away. But if they had caught me I would have joined the others in that shallow forest grave. . . .

I had some food, warmer clothes, and decent boots; another three days and I was again in Delatyn. Almost the first thing I saw was Grandmother's house, a mere shell; it had been ransacked and then half demolished. I did not stop to search for any of our possessions, I knew it was no use. I went to the Ukrainian's house, approaching it from the back, after night-fall. As soon as he saw me he said, "You mustn't stay here, Emil. Not for a minute. They've killed all the Jews they could find; they're still hunting for the few that escaped."

"But my grandmother . . ."

"I'm sorry."

He told me that one of his neighbours had seen Grandmother slip into his house and told the Gestapo about her. They dragged her out and pushed her among the crowd that was being driven to the market-place. She could not walk fast enough, like so many of the old and the sick. They shot her down in the street. Then they loaded her body on a cart and . . .

I could not blame the Ukrainian, even though I wasn't sure whether he hadn't betrayed Grandmother himself. And if I had been with her I wouldn't be alive myself. Though he urged me again to leave at once, I stayed another two days in Delatyn, sleeping in a ruined cellar, going out only at night-time. I talked to one or two of the Jews who had somehow survived. They told me that more than fifteen hundred people had been taken by the Germans; the Gestapo used dogs to ferret them out, even offered small rewards to anybody leading them to their hiding-places. Several of my cousins and almost twenty of my more distant relatives perished on that single day.

There was nothing I could do in that half-deserted village and on the third night I started out again for Kolomyja, keep-ing to the forest and the fields, avoiding the villages, again stealing what food I could. I did not meet a single human being until the outskirts of the town and I reached our home without mishap.

9

The workshop of which Father was the technical head needed trained workers and it wasn't difficult for him to get the German supervisor to accept me as one of his assistants. At least my college education was paying off; I could handle the turning and polishing machines without difficulty.

There were seventeen of us in the workshop—two Poles and fifteen Jews. Our working day started at seven in the morning and lasted twelve hours. For this we were given a pound of bread twice a week and two pounds of flour once a week. We would have starved except for Janek Seibald, my cousin, who lived with us and who had been a mill-owner before the war. Now the Germans had put him in charge of a flour-mill and he was able to smuggle out small quantities now and again.

Apart from repairing any vehicle the District Commandant's office and the Gestapo brought to the shop, we had to make the large cylinders for the rolling mills. We were supplied with ample material to make these because they were needed to keep the mills going. So after seven o'clock in the evening we stayed on and made some extra ones which the Ukrainians sold for us. Each took about four hours and we got very little sleep; we would make two or three in a night. But one morning our German supervisor (he was a *Volksdeutscher* from Silesia and knew Polish quite well) noticed that the machine was still warm. He asked whether anybody had worked overtime.

I thought he would find out anyhow and I said, "I made some extra cylinders for a Ukrainian."

"How much did he pay you?" he asked.

"Nothing," I replied. "He gave me two loaves of bread for two cylinders."

The German looked angry and I began to feel uneasy.

"Only two loaves of bread?" he said furiously. "Why, the *Schweinehund*!"

"Yes, sir, that was all."

He came closer to me. I thought he was going to hit me, but instead he said, "Well, listen to me, Jew. *I* will send you another Ukrainian who will give you *two sacks of flour* for each cylinder. You give me one and you can keep the other. All right?"

Of course I said it was all right. So we went on doing extra work, and this helped us very much because food was getting very scarce. As the Silesian got his cut, he did not bother us at all.

He was like most people, neither particularly good nor particularly bad. If he could earn something on the side he was very glad to; otherwise he left us pretty much alone.

Not that the German authorities were so tolerant. By October 1941, not long after the Delatyn massacre, all Jews had to

45

wear white armbands with a blue Star of David. In the following month we had to give up our home in town and all Jews were moved into the newly established ghetto. We were put into a tiny three-room cottage (it was more like a hut), which we shared with two other families. We had passes so we could go to the workshop every morning and had to return to the ghetto in the evenings.

Food became scarcer and scarcer and not even Janek Seibald could bring home enough from the mill to help us, especially as people were often searched when entering the ghetto. The ghetto itself grew into two sections—the Little and the Main Ghetto. As starvation threatened, people paid a hundred zloty for a couple of pounds of potatoes (the pre-war price had been about half a zloty); some mixed nettles with maize-flour. And the population of the ghetto grew, in spite of many deaths, as all Jews from the neighbouring villages were being concentrated here. Those who still had some money left bought what food they could from the Ukrainians who lived in the Aryan quarter adjoining our place, or, when money became worthless, they bartered their few remaining possessions, clothes or valuables, for a little flour or some soup-bones.

About this time a young Pole called Wojcielch Migdal with whom I had made friends came to me and said that the Gestapo was preparing for a large-scale "Jew-hunt" to discover and drive into the ghetto all those who were still outside, and then would begin to liquidate the ghetto itself. I told as many people as I could and many hid in the various cellars and underground bunkers. Next day Father and I went, as usual, to the workshop; we had no choice, for our absence would have been noticed at once and, of course, we needed the food we earned with our work. I must explain that the workshops were all within the ghetto, but their entrance was on the non-Jewish side. While we were on our way to work we heard shooting from the direction of the so-called Little Ghetto. We got to the workshop without any mishap and did our daily stint, though waiting and listening uneasily for any tell-tale sounds. Around noon some Gestapo men came in and demanded from the German supervisor a list of the workers. One of them was called Hubermann, an SS *Oberscharfuehrer*, marked with the same duelling scar as the Gestapo commander in the Bukovinka forest. Our supervisor, the same man who was our partner in our illegal manufacture of cylinders, declared that all the people in the workshop were specialists, highly trained and essential for the work which was being done for the Gestapo and the ordinary *Schutzpolizei*. Of course, we pretended to work harder than ever, though it was not easy while the bargaining over our fate continued. But Hubermann and his men left and we went on working, not finishing until almost midnight and then spending the night in the workshop, bedding down on some sacking, sleeping fitfully.

Next morning we found out that the entire Little Ghetto had been liquidated: its inhabitants were taken to Scheparowce and executed in the forest with the usual thorough, efficient German methods. We realized that it was only a question of time before the entire population of the ghetto was exterminated. So we decided to build an underground shelter beneath our little house. For three weeks we toiled every evening, excavating a large enough bunker, nine feet deep, to hide all of us.

At the same time we began to store some non-perishable food which we got from a Pole called Tomaszkiewicz, who was honest enough to help us. We gave him whatever clothes or other things we could spare; he could have kept it all or could have denounced us to the Germans, but he did neither and became our link with the outside world. We had agreed that at the first sign of danger we would all hide in the underground shelter; but if someone was caught outside or managed to slip through the net into the non-Jewish part of the town, he or she would get news to Tomaszkiewicz, so that we could find out where we could meet again, or at least keep in touch.

After the liquidation of the Little Ghetto the official distribution of food stopped almost entirely and we became hungrier and hungrier. The only way to obtain what little we could manage to scrounge was to have it smuggled in from the "Aryan" side for very high prices, which few could afford. For a couple of pounds of wheat or barley the Ukrainians demanded and got shoes, overcoats, and whole suits. Some of them acquired the most elaborate wardrobes within a few weeks.

The second wave of liquidating the Kolomyja ghetto came early in the New Year, the year 1942. Once again we were lucky. The supervisor of our workshop had given Father and myself special passes which were signed by Hubermann. On the day of the mass executions we were told not to leave our little house, and, of course, all the others stayed inside with us. But that day hundreds of our friends and some of our relatives perished.

10

The winter was long and sapped our strength; we thought it would never end and every day was a struggle against hunger and cold. There were fewer people in the ghetto now, but that did not improve the food situation, for most of them had nothing left to barter with.

In the early spring Hubermann sent for my father and asked him whether he could obtain some essential spares for their vehicles. They had the proper requisition forms, but could not find the things anywhere. They knew through the supervisor of the workshop that Father had good connections in the Cracow district and told him to see what he could do. Of course, Father knew that it would be immensely difficult to get the items, which in those days were worth their weight in gold, but he also realized that this was probably his only chance to get a pass to travel to Tarnow, to see Mother, from whom we received occasional messages and one or two letters.

After some discussion and various threats that the members of his family left behind in Kolomyja would be instantly liquidated if he failed to return, Father was given the travel documents for Cracow and Tarnow. Trains were in service again, though neither frequent nor regular. He did get to our hometown, where he found Mother much aged and thinner, but otherwise unharmed. In the western part of Poland the deportations and mass executions had not yet started, and while all Jews had been conscripted for forced labour, they could lead a comparatively normal and peaceful existence, though no-one could tell for how long.

Father had to sell a greater part of our still remaining possessions in Tarnow in order to obtain the spare parts required by the Gestapo. (German occupation marks would have only bought a fraction of them.) When he returned to Kolomyja with his precious cargo and some food for us Hubermann and the others were amazed at his success. As a reward, they promised him that in a month's time he could go to Tarnow again and could bring Mother back.

As it happened, all this took longer than expected and when Mother's travel papers arrived Father was not allowed to leave Kolomyja. There was urgent work to be done and the Germans said there was no need for him to go, they would arrange for Mother's journey. Father did not believe them. He passed Mother's documents on to Tomaszkiewicz, asking him to send them on to Dr Firbel, the Polish doctor who was our landlord in Tarnow and who could then give them to Mother.

It was too late.

On June 10th, 1942, the Germans began the liquidation of the Jews in Tarnow. Because Mother had the documents issued by the Gestapo in Kolomyja she decided to leave the ghetto and get to the railway station. She asked Dr Firbel to accompany her. He refused to walk with her, but promised that he would follow her at a little distance until she actually got on the train and then send news to Tomaszkiewicz about her safe departure.

All went well until they arrived outside the station. There the police stopped Mother. She showed all her documents, which were in perfect order.

"They're no good today," a Gestapo man told her curtly and tore them up. She wept and called for Dr Firbel, but he was terrified to get involved with the troubles of a Jewess. They dragged her to a siding and put her on a train that soon left for Mielec. We had no more news about her, but most of the people from Mielec were sent to Maidanek and died in the gas chambers. Dr Firbel got word to Tomaszkiewicz, telling him what happened, but we didn't get that message until a long time afterwards.

Perhaps it was better that we didn't. For several months we believed that Mother was safe and well and were grateful that she did not have to share our own plight, which soon got worse.

Strangely enough, I remember that during those weeks I dreamt of her several times. She scolded me for letting my hair grow long and not washing it regularly and tried to sew some buttons on my ragged shirt, only she couldn't seem to get the needle threaded and that made her cry. She was so real, so tangibly close, that when I woke up I spoke her name, and, falling asleep again, I saw her once more with the needle and the thread. For her the separation from us, from Father and

Martha and myself, was a very cruel punishment, and I think she must have gone to her death unresisting and uncomplaining. But she is with me as much as if she were still alive, or had only died a few months ago, though almost thirty years have passed since they stopped her on the very threshold of joining her family.

11

It was the end of June 1942, hot and dusty; there had been no rain for weeks. One afternoon when Father and I were particularly nervous and tense (because we were waiting for news about Mother), Wojcielch Migdal came to the workshop, drew me into a corner and said, "Emil, try to get away; within the next few days the whole ghetto will be liquidated. Don't ask me how I know, but I *do* know."

Of course I believed him and passed on the warning as quickly as possible. Those I told hid in their various cellars and bunkers; some, though not many, managed to get into the non-Jewish, adjoining quarter of Kolomyja.

When we returned that evening from the workshop everything was still quiet and peaceful. Some people even abused Father and me for spreading unnecessary panic. We felt like the boy who cried wolf, but then we remembered that the wolf did come in the end.

We went to bed and slept until about three o'clock in the morning, when we heard shots, screams, and the tramp of feet. We got up quickly and dressed. The shots sounded now much closer, almost in the next houses. At the last moment I managed to push Janek Seibald's mother into our hiding-place.

A few seconds later an axe splintered the front door of our little house; a Ukrainian and a Gestapo man came in. The German recognized Father and told the Ukrainian not to hurt us. The house wasn't searched, but we were told to get out and make our way to the large, empty space in the middle of the ghetto which was called the Parade Ground. The Ukrainian stayed with us. As we walked there we saw many people being dragged brutally from the huts and houses, women by their hair, men by their legs or twisted arms. Those who showed the slightest resistance or were slow to move were being beaten without mercy. We came across several who lay on the ground with gaping skulls, their heads split open with axes, others who had been shot where they stumbled or fell.

The Ukrainian who was our escort did not touch us; he only told us gruffly to hurry. It was about a quarter to four in the morning when we got to the Parade Ground, where men, women, and children were separated, counted, and re-counted. We stayed there until noon, when the German supervisor of the workshop appeared; he soon realized that he could do nothing for us and, with a brief glance but without a word to us, he disappeared.

We had to stand in the blazing sun for more than twelve hours that day without food or a drop of water. Then they marched us to the goods depot of Kolomyja. Again there was a lot of beating and many were killed on the way because the old and sick had been much weakened by the long wait in the heat. They drove us through the gates, some fifteen hundred men, women, and children. The train stood ready—freight-cars with small, heavily barred windows or, rather, a single window for each.

I noticed, however, that one of the freight-cars near the end of the train did not have bars but only some wooden slats nailed across it. I was close to my father and my sister was just behind me, so I said, "Father, that's the one we must get into if at all possible." He was a little dazed and asked, "What is it, Emil?" I had to repeat it and someone else heard me, which meant that there was an awful jostling and pushing to get into that particular car. So much so that once we had boarded it (all the members of the three families in our Kolomyja ghetto home were with us) it was locked and barred behind us. Instead of the average forty or fifty, about a hundred or more crowded into that space, packed like sardines so that we couldn't even move our hands. It was hotter than in a baking oven and it was a long time before the train started. Everybody tried to get to the window, or at least nearer to it, which was, of course, impossible. The children screamed and cried, but no-one could move an inch to help them. Then people began to faint and collapse, only, of course, there was no space for them to fall, and those who did were trampled to death. In their death agony some bit the legs of the people closest to them, the dying ones' bowels and bladders emptied, and the stink and miasmatic steam rose like thick fog. About a dozen died in our car before

51

the train even began to move, and by the end we counted forty dead.

It was almost evening before I was able to inch my way to the window. Apart from the slats, it was also covered with barbed wire, and I began to twist the wire aside, barely noticing that it lacerated my hands. Outside I could just see the armed guard, who was riding on the footplate that ran all round the freight-car. As he noticed me, he asked, "Where's that pretty blonde?"

I knew at once that he meant Nuka Horowitz, who was certainly a very beautiful young girl, a natural, blue-eyed blonde, though by now, poor girl, she didn't look her best. (She lived in a house near to ours in the ghetto and I knew her well.)

It turned out that the guard, an Austrian, had seen her a few times and also had noticed her when she got into that terrible crowded place with us. I told the people around me to find her and bring her to the window. It took almost an hour before they passed her from hand to hand, lifting her over the corpses, until she stood beside me. As soon as she saw the guard she begged him to give us some water. He handed her his canteen, which was full, but she had hardly got hold of it when some-one tore it from her hand and a wild struggle began. In the end no-one was able to drink a single drop—it was all spilled uselessly.

I stepped a little to the side and let Nuka talk to the Austrian. "Please," she said, "won't you open the door? Won't you let us escape? . . . I'll do anything if you help us. . . . I'm too young to die."

"I can't do that," I heard him saying. "I've a wife and three kids, and I'd be shot if I disobeyed my orders."

But he suddenly disappeared from sight, moving to the other end of the footplate. We made use of this chance (it was now getting dark), and with Nuka and Janek Seibald, I succeeded in removing all the barbed wire and then breaking the slats, which were not very thick, so that we could do this quickly. The train was moving at about thirty miles an hour. We knew we had a chance. The window was too high up to climb and jump through it, but if someone was lifted he could be eased through the opening feet first, aimed in the direction in which we were travelling, which would give him a reasonable chance to fall free. In order to reach the window, we had to pile up some corpses as a sort of shelf or ladder; but we had no hesitation in doing that. It could not hurt them any longer and it did help us, the living.

I was the first to stick my head through the window. A moment later I felt a blow, a glancing rather than a heavy one, on my head. It was the guard, using the butt of his rifle, but he hadn't really hurt me and I persisted. We lifted up a young man and manipulated him through the window until he disappeared in the darkness. A few shots were fired—the guard had earlier told Nuka that a machine-gun was mounted on the roof of the last car and he was afraid that if he opened the door he would be gunned down himself—but that did not deter us. Another man went through the opening. Then we picked a woman. She was still hanging on by one hand when I saw that the guard pressed his rifle against her head and seemed to fire. Maybe he had an empty magazine, for she cried to us, "Push me, push me, I am all right!" We did what she wanted and we understood that the Austrian was only pretending to shoot at us so that he shouldn't get into trouble. Whoever managed to get through that window had a reasonable chance.

I told my father that it was his turn now, for by then Nuka and Janek were both gone, but he was sitting close to a small opening, breathing deeply, and he told me to get Martha out first and then jump myself—he would follow a little later when he had collected his strength. I started to argue and he shouted at me, "I am your father! Do as you're told!"

Martha was in the middle of the car and it took me quite a while until I extricated her. She fainted by the time I got her to the window, and when we lifted her I had to slap her face hard to bring her back to consciousness, or she might have been killed when we got her through the opening. After she had gone—it was now about 2 A.M.—Father told me to walk along the track when I got out, in our present direction and if we should miss each other send a message to Tomaszkiewicz about where we had landed. I kissed him, and then I was also lifted to the window, feeling the cool night air on my face, hearing the wheels as I launched myself into space. I landed rather heavily and rolled down the embankment, but I wasn't hurt, only a little bruised, because I had coiled myself into a large ball as I was falling and came down upon my shoulders and arms.

It was dark as I started back along the track to find my sister. On the way I came upon several dead and wounded people.

Some had been killed by the fall, others by the SS bullets, for as soon as they had noticed that people were trying to escape they started to fire at them. But they couldn't stop the train, which by now was many miles away; even its tail-lights had disappeared. I wondered and worried about Father. I asked some of the wounded whether they had seen Martha, but no-one had, and anyhow it was pretty dark to recognize anybody.

Then I heard groans and someone called out. I bent down and recognized a friend from the Kolomyja ghetto, a boy of nineteen, son of a chemist. He looked up as I spoke his name. Both his legs had been severed by the wheels of the train; he had jumped clumsily and the swing had carried him right on the tracks. But he was conscious and his brain seemed to be quite clear.

"Listen, Emil . . .," he said, his voice faint but calm, "I'm done for. . . . My parents jumped out after me. . . . If you see them along the track tell them where I am."

"Can't I do anything?"

"No, you can't," he cut me short. "Just tell them."

As I straightened I saw two shadowy figures behind me. They were his parents and they must have heard him. His mother gave a sort of whimper; his father bent over him. The boy said, "You see how it is with me. You can't help me. But I know you have cyanide, Papa. Please give me some, so I can die without much pain . . . and save yourselves before the Germans come back."

Of course they wouldn't do that, though I knew they had some capsules. I had a few, too; most people in the ghetto had managed to hide some quick-acting poison. Ours had been brought back by Father when he went to Tarnow; he got them from Dr Firbel, I think.

The crippled boy and his parents began to argue, though he was getting weaker and weaker. I left them because I felt I could not possibly help, and continued walking back along the embankment, softly whistling the tune which was our regular signal. I must have walked about a mile and a half when at last I heard a faint answering whistle from a roadside ditch. It was Martha. She was only half-conscious; her face and one hand had been cut. But even in her half-conscious state she had responded to my whistling. I helped her to her feet and said, "Come on, we must get away. . . ."

54

Suddenly she began to shiver and whimper and tried to break away from me.

"What's the matter?" I asked.

"There . . . there are lamps there . . . the Germans are signalling . . . we must hide . . . we can't go on."

I looked, but there were no lamps, only some fireflies in the warm summer night. She was still in a state of shock, but I forced her to start walking, in the opposite direction, back towards the spot where I had landed. I knew that we had to get to the nearest town, where it would be easier to hide and find food than in the open country.

Before long we came across the chemist's son. He was dead. His father must have given him the cyanide after all, for he was alone and seemed at peace. I tried to keep the sight from Martha, but she was still too dazed to notice anyway.

A little farther along the line we came upon a railway guard's hut. I told my sister to wait outside because her face was still covered in blood and she looked much worse than her actual condition. I knocked and went in and asked the guard, an elderly man, whether he could give me a little water and food. He already knew that a train packed with Jews had passed. He asked me whether I was alone. I told him my sister was waiting outside.

"Bring her in," he said. I hesitated, but he looked kind enough and I had no choice but to trust him. So I brought Martha in, and when he saw the blood on her face and head he said, "Wash yourself, have a drink of water, take this half-loaf, then run! Chodorov is only two miles from here. Don't go along the track, because the Ukrainians who live near by will certainly denounce you, nor across the fields, because the shepherds will do the same. Keep to the far side of the woods, then you'll be safe."

We thanked him and called ourselves lucky that he was a Pole and human. After Martha had washed off the blood we saw that her wounds were all superficial and would heal quickly enough; she combed her hair so that the cuts and bruises were not so evident. The water we drank, almost a couple of pints each, and the bread we shared gave us new strength. Martha asked about Father and I lied to her, telling her that he jumped just after me and that we would meet him in Chodorov, for I did not want her to worry.

It was still dark when we set out again.

12

In Chodorov there was an open ghetto; the Jews all lived together in one quarter, but it was not enclosed with barbed wire. Of course, when we came into the place they noticed us and began to ask us where we had come from. By noon there were twenty-six of us who had all escaped from the train, though only three from our freight-car. A good many more had jumped, but the others hadn't reached Chodorov.

The Jewish Council, which was headed by a local lawyer and which was appointed by the Germans, gave us food and shelter in the synagogue. Martha felt very weak and lay down on a mattress, falling fast asleep, but I decided to go out into the town and discover what was happening. Before long I overheard people discussing agitatedly that the Germans were demanding that all those who escaped from the train should be delivered up to them, and in addition five hundred local Jews, to punish them for having sheltered us. This discussion took place outside the lawyer's house, which was not very far from the synagogue.

I ran back immediately and woke Martha. She was exhausted and I had great difficulty in forcing her to follow me. By then it was evening again. I half carried, half supported her along the street. I had decided to go to the lawyer's house; if anybody, he would do his utmost to save himself and there we too would be temporarily safe.

We had no sooner left the synagogue than the Ukrainian police began to drag people from it and round up the five hundred local Jews. They also started to search for underground shelters and hiding-places. I went to the lawyer, who had a well-camouflaged and capacious cellar, and said to him, "Take my sister in!"

He was a small man with glasses and terribly nervous. "I can't," he said. "There is no room."

"There is always room for one extra person," I said. "Take her without me."

He was thinking fast; I could see the conflicting emotions in his face.

"All right," he said, for he saw that I was determined. "But then you come, too."

"No, I won't. I'll take care of myself."

"But why don't you? ..."

"Listen," I told him, "if you betray my sister I'll go to the Germans and tell them that you're hiding other people here and they'll take you and your family too."

"If you do that you'll be committing suicide yourself."

"I don't care. And don't you believe that I wouldn't do it. Stop arguing; there isn't much time left."

He took Martha and disappeared with his family. All night and all next day I hid on the flat roof of a house opposite, watching the lawyer's house, without food or water. I saw how people were being dragged out of the houses, beaten, and driven like cattle to the station. But no-one went into the lawyer's house and no-one came out. The round-up went on all night and most of the next day, but then it became quiet and I fell asleep. Then I heard people talking in Yiddish and I knew that at least for the time being there was no danger. I climbed from the roof and went into the lawyer's house just as he and his family were emerging from their hiding-place. Martha was also there. Some people came into the house and, when they saw us, began to gesticulate and shout. "Five hundred of our people are being taken away, but the strangers were hidden and kept safe!"

As I listened to the talk I knew that we couldn't stay any longer in Chodorov, that we had to leave at once. I told Martha to follow me, pretending we were just having a talk. We rounded the corner, I took her arm and we began to run. As we reached the next street a middle-aged man suddenly stepped forward. He was wearing the white armband with the blue star.

"Are you Emil Brigg?" he asked.

"Yes. Who are you?"

"Never mind. I've been following you, but I couldn't get to you—too many people around. I have a message for you from Tomaszkiewicz."

I looked at him. If he had wanted to denounce us to the Germans he wouldn't have waited for us in this lonely spot.

"What message?" I asked cautiously.

"From your father. He's got away from the Germans. He's in Stryj. He says get there when you can."

57

"But—where in Stryj? I don't know the place."

"The message didn't say. But you'll find him, I dare say."

There were some footsteps close by and he darted back into a doorway, motioning for us to move on. We did.

13

A few miles outside Chodorov we came to a little village and I went into an isolated farmhouse. I asked the farmer whether he could let us stay there and work for him without wages, just for our keep. There was a great shortage of farmhands, as so many people had been sent to Germany to forced labour. He must have suspected something, but he said it was all right. I said I would leave Martha with him and would come back to start work in a week. He didn't like that very much, but he agreed in the end. I didn't want my sister to make the long and difficult journey before I knew how things were in Stryj and whether Father was really there. I had found out in the meantime that Stryj had a large ghetto and a labour camp run by the *Wehrmacht*, not by the SS, which might give us a better chance. Martha was a little unhappy at being left alone, but I promised to come back to fetch her as soon as possible, and finally she let me go.

Only I didn't get very far. Outside the next village two Ukrainian policemen suddenly appeared from the roadside bushes. They had guns and they covered me from both sides; I had no chance to fight, even if I had had any weapons, nor to run away. I was wearing blue overalls, without the Jewish armband, but of course I had no pass, no documents. At first they argued whether they should kill me on the spot, but they decided that whatever they would get for my clothes would be less than the bounty the Germans paid for any run-away Jew they found. They dragged me all the way back to the Chodorov railway station, where they handed me over to the Gestapo. They were still busy loading another deportation train with the five hundred they had taken from the Chodorov ghetto and they simply pushed me into the nearest group. This time there were no windows one could break: all of them were strongly barred. There were fewer people in the freight-car, but even so it was closely packed. There was much shouting and people were being beaten. At last the train was loaded, I found myself in a car which had only men, and the train started almost at once.

The journey was much shorter this time; before nightfall we arrived in Lwow. We were lined up along the siding and the Gestapo men walked up and down, picking out the young men and women who looked strong and reasonably healthy. I was chosen, though nobody knew for what; we only guessed that it would be for work. Then two German soldiers and five Jewish policemen escorted us into the large Janovski camp, where we spent the night without food, although we managed to get a little water. I was watching for an opportunity to escape, but there was none: men and dogs patrolled around the huts all night.

At five o'clock in the morning we were herded outside. I was in a group of twenty. Again it was under strong escort that they led us out of the camp to start work in a factory. The Jewish policemen warned us not to try to escape, as they were responsible for everybody and would have to stop us because they would be punished severely if they helped us in any way.

We had now reached the main gate of the factory. Just inside there was a paling with a door that was open. I moved very fast and as the group marched in stepped behind the door and pressed myself against the paling. There was just enough space to squeeze myself in. There I waited. When the group was well inside the factory area and no alarm had been raised I slipped from my hiding-place. There was a terribly strong temptation to run, but I forced myself to walk out into the street, strolling slowly and calmly along. I could feel the sweat gathering on my back, but I walked several hundred yards at the same pace. I was lucky again, for no-one noticed me. There were few people about and they all seemed to be intent on their own affairs.

I did not know Lwow well, though I had been there once before. I continued walking until I reached the suburbs. There I asked a woman who had three small children with her the way to Stryj. Fortunately she was able and willing to give me at least the general direction. I reached a near-by copse, and there I hid all day, for I was determined not to risk being caught again.

As I started out I began to think about all the chances I had taken and the people I had met. Some had been helpful enough, like the railway guard or the farmer with whom I had left Martha. People were different and they acted for different motives. Some helped because they were paid, others because they were given clothes or other scarce and precious articles, and there were a few—a very few—who helped out of kindness, out of humanity. During the three years of our tribulations we have even met Jews who betrayed others, sometimes out of fear, sometimes out of revenge, sometimes because they wanted to make money or save their own skins. I only hoped that I would not meet any of this sort.

I made a long circuit of the city to avoid the German patrols, who were always watching out for Jews, black marketeers, deserters from the labour corps around the big cities. It was a Friday on which I started out from Lwow. Later I followed the railway track, until I came to the river Dniester, which was very wide and deep, swollen by the recent rains. There were only two ways to cross it, either by the bridge, which was, of course, guarded day and night by the Germans, or in one of the little fishing-boats which the Ukrainians and the Poles kept tied up on the bank. First I reconnoitred the bridge, hoping that there would be a changing of the guards and I could slip across. But the bridge was almost two hundred yards long and I saw the sentries walking up and down its entire length all the time. When they were relieved the new lot continued immediately; there wasn't a single moment when I could have crossed. So I moved away along the river until I came to a small village. I spent the whole day there, watching and waiting for the fishermen to go back home after their day's work. A few minutes after they had all disappeared I took one of the boats and managed to cross without oars (which the villagers had carried off). The current carried me about a mile downstream before I landed on the far bank. Then I started again upstream to get away as quickly and as far as possible from the spot where I had borrowed the boat.

That night I slipped into another village and stole a few potatoes. I went into some woods and made a little fire and roasted them. I couldn't have done that in daytime, for someone would have noticed the smoke. I ate some potatoes and kept some for the next day; even though there is nothing more horrible than cold potatoes, badly charred and without salt. To

60

this very day I cannot touch roast potatoes. I lived on them for two days and was getting more and more sick of them.

On the third day I met an old Pole who was driving a hay-cart. I called out to him and asked whether he would give me a lift, for I was very tired and hungry. By now I began to feel like a man who had fallen into a wolf-trap, climbed out with great difficulty and effort, only to fall into another and another. The old man nodded and I climbed up. He was lonely and bored and began to talk. He asked where I had come from and I said I was from Lwow, looking for work because there was none to be had in the city. He told me there was no work at his farm, there wasn't enough to do for himself and his family, the Germans took most of what they produced, barely leaving him seed-corn.

Then he looked at me and asked, "Aren't you a Jew?"

I was silent for a while, then I said, "What if I were?"

"I'd give you something to eat and then tell you to make yourself scarce. I don't want to be hanged for helping Jews."

He pulled a small parcel of sausages and bread from under the box, handed it to me, and told me to get off. When I thanked him he just shook his head and the haycart swayed on, disappearing round a bend.

I went on. The food the old man had given me didn't last long. I was sleeping in the open, getting soaked by the heavy dew. Mostly I slept in the daytime and walked at night. Then I would slip into the farmyards and steal eggs from the hencoops. I drew water from the wells. But when I got to Stryj there was another problem: I was filthy after almost six days on the road, I had started to sprout a beard, and my overalls were stained and torn. If I had gone into the town in this condition I would have immediately been recognized as a fugitive. So I waited until nightfall, and when it was dark I approached the ghetto, spending the night on its outskirts. In the morning I watched from a secure hiding-place and saw people going out to work. There were no Ukrainian guards, only the Jewish police. I jumped over a fence and went to the camp council, telling them how I had escaped from the deportation train of Kolomyja, but not saying anything about Chodorov or my sister. They gave me soap, and at last I could have a proper wash and also got some second-hand but serviceable clothes.

"Look," they said, "you're young and in good condition. Why don't you join the camp police?"

"No, I couldn't do that," I said.

"But why not? You'd get decent clothes, boots, regular rations."

"I just couldn't. I don't want to help the Germans in any way that brings suffering to other Jews . . . I don't want to do their dirty work."

They tried to persuade me, but I wouldn't budge from my decision. "Very well," they said, "then you'll have to go to the labour camp."

"All right. Where is it?"

They explained that there was a camp a mile and a half from the ghetto in which about fifteen hundred Jews lived. They all worked for the *Wehrmacht*, building portable barracks and huts. There were two shifts, from 5 A.M. to 5 P.M. and from 5 P.M. to 5 A.M. Our working norms were strictly set: when I started I had to hammer in two thousand nails daily, fastening the wall and roof panels to the framework. For this work we were paid a loaf of bread weekly, half a glass of molasses daily, a mug of coffee in the morning (unsweetened), and a plate of soup in the evening. If we had any money or valuables left we could buy extra rations from the Poles.

The first day I had to find my way around and get my work schedule arranged. But I began to ask about my father. The ghetto was in a bad state of nerves just then; the day before my arrival the Germans had rounded up four hundred people whom they took away; no-one knew whether they were moved to another camp or executed. Work had been suspended while these were picked, but when it was resumed I asked some of the workers whether anybody knew a man called Brigg from Kolomyja.

"Is he a new one?" someone asked.

"Yes."

"Go into the second workshop, he may be there."

I went and there was Father, working away busily on a lathe. We did not have much time to celebrate our reunion. After he had patted me on the back he asked me, "Do you have any cigarettes?"

I said I had and offered him the pack. He took one and looked at me. "Aren't you having one, too?"

I had been smoking for the last year or so, but had kept it a secret from Father; I thought he would disapprove, for he had always told me I mustn't smoke before I was eighteen. So I

62

grinned and took a cigarette; he offered me a match. We sat there, smoking, for a quarter of an hour, and I felt that he had now accepted me as a grown-up. It was a strange, happy feeling and I forgot how tired I had been after my long cross-country hike.

I asked Father why he had come to Stryj, and he explained that he had heard about a labour camp where he had a friend named Lackritz; he thought that this man would help him. He had first sent word to Tomaszkiewicz, as we had agreed (and we did, of course, get the message in Chodorov), then he set out for Stryj, walking for several days. When he got there he found that Lackritz was in charge of the carpentry section of the labour camp. Father just started to work there without telling anybody anything. This wasn't difficult, for the labour camp was entirely run by the Jewish police, there were no SS men, no roll-call; as long as the work was done, the huts and barracks turned out in the expected quantity, they left us alone.

Lackritz got Father an identity card and when I arrived I got one too, which enabled me not only to stay in the labour camp but to enter the ghetto whenever I wanted to, which proved most useful later. We agreed that I should fetch Martha from the farmer with whom I had left her. We couldn't get her into the labour camp, for that would have needed a special permit which only the German in charge of the whole operation, a *Volksdeutscher* called Kadziora, could sign, and he charged so much that we couldn't possibly afford it. But Lackritz gave Father some money, and that bought a bed in a room in the ghetto where Martha would be able to stay with four other girls.

It was Lackritz too who covered up for my absence when I set out again for Chodorov: he reported me sick. This time the journey took only four days, for I knew exactly the best route, what danger-points to avoid, and where to cross the river. I reached the farm in the evening and waited until I could call my sister with our signal. She told me that the farmer had treated her well, though she had had to work very hard. She already knew about Father and me having met in Stryj because Tomaszkiewicz had managed to get a message to her, and she had even sent a letter to the Stryj ghetto. I told her to get her things together and slip out when everybody was asleep in the farmhouse, as we couldn't risk the farmer keeping her back by force or even asking where she was going. She managed to do as I told her and a little after midnight we were on our way. Again the journey took us four days. It was now July and food was easier to scavenge. We reached Stryj without any mishap. I took Martha to the ghetto, where she already had her place prepared, and I returned to the labour camp. My absence had been carefully covered and I started work again without trouble.

14

All through the summer and the early autumn we lived and worked in Stryj, and though life was hard, it was far more pleasant and bearable than it had been during the previous two years. I was able to visit Martha often in the ghetto, we could buy extra food, and Lackritz, as my father's friend, helped us in many ways.

It was soon after my second arrival in Stryj, when I brought my sister from the farm near Chodorov, that I met Olga. She was one of Martha's room-mates, a slim and delicate brunette, daughter of a local merchant. She was shy and quiet, but I managed to make her talk, and within a couple of weeks we had become lovers. It would have been different in peace-time, there would have been a long courtship, and our parents would have been concerned with our plans, our engagement, and our ultimate marriage. But there were no weddings in the ghetto and we young people felt that we were living on borrowed time, that any day the Germans might decide to liquidate the ghetto, as they had done in Kolomyja, Chodorov, and so many other places. During the long summer nights Olga and I used to meet in a store shed which we called our "love-nest"; every broken crate and every rusty tool we renamed a "sofa" or "an armchair" or "a mahogany wardrobe"; we furnished that small, grimy place in our imagination as if it were a luxury apartment, and we had long discussions about whether we had chosen the right colour for the curtains or whether we should "buy" a Persian or a Chinese carpet for the living-room. And, of course, we made plans for after the war, where we would live and how many children we would have. We had our lovers' quarrels, too, for Olga could be jealous if I looked at another

64

girl or joked with some woman; but we always made it up and the reconciliation was worth the quarrel.

One night we were together in our shed. We had made love and Olga had gone to sleep in my arms when shouting and banging woke us up. The shed had a small window and we could see lights outside. Olga began to tremble.

"The Germans . . . they're going to take us away."

I told her to be quiet and moved to the window; some Ukrainians and SS men were going from building to building. I noticed that all the people whom they dragged out were women. I did not want Olga to know, but she was now standing beside me and it was too late to lie to her.

"Give it to me," she said, shivering and crying. "You promised you would . . . if they came . . ."

I hesitated. It was true that we had made a pact: if ever we were in a hopeless situation together we would swallow one of the cyanide capsules of which I still had a small supply.

"Wait . . .," I begged her. "They may not come in here."

Her sobs became louder; I felt that she might become hysterical.

"No, no, I want it . . . please."

There was no other way to quieten her, so I gave her one of the capsules.

"Olga . . . you must promise . . . don't do anything foolish. . . . I'll slip away now, but if they take you I promise I'll get you away. Promise!"

She nodded, a little calmer. I kissed her and opened the back door of the shed (I had oiled the hinges so that it moved noiselessly). It was close to the low wall of the ghetto and I vaulted over it, then flattened and waited.

Inside the rounding-up of women continued for another half an hour, then it became quiet. It was perhaps the worst half-hour in my life. But no-one went into the shed. I waited another ten minutes to be sure, then I went back to her.

She was dead.

For many days after Olga's suicide I walked about, I ate and drank, worked and slept, as if I were some robot which had been wound up and would go on mechanically, without consciousness, until it ran down. I blamed myself for leaving her, for giving her the cyanide, and that made it even worse. I was, when the numbness wore off, filled with such fury, such seething anger, directed partly against myself, that I felt I would go mad if I had no chance of doing something soon to revenge myself for Olga's death.

It was September now, and one evening Yankel came to me and told me about Stach Babij.

15

In the early thirties Stach Babij was a farmer, and later became a forester. He was a Ukrainian and he did not get on well with his superiors, who were all Poles. He beat up one of them in a quarrel and lost his job. He turned poacher, and when they tried to confiscate his gun he became a bandit.

Until the outbreak of the war he followed this profession, living as an outlaw in the great forests, visiting his family occasionally in the village, which was called Babijuska (the whole population belonged to one clan), where he had a lot of brothers and sisters, all of whom lived in the same place. He continued poaching and committed an occasional robbery. The Polish gendarmes were hunting him for years, but could never catch him. The Russians, when they occupied Eastern Poland, did the same, but never even got near him: he knew the country too well and had hundreds of loyal allies who warned him if any enemy approached. After the Nazi invasion the Germans destroyed the whole of Babijuska and deported his entire clan. That is when he decided to start a war against them; from a regular bandit he turned into a partisan leader. And it is a measure of his skill, courage, and cunning that he survived the whole war—and, as far as I know, he is still alive today.

Stach Babij was a man of medium height, but with immensely broad shoulders, long arms, and prodigious strength. He had a handsome face and a large shock of reddish-brown hair, a bristling moustache, and a well-trimmed beard. He was a strange mixture of bravery and cruelty, of kindness and sudden, berserk rages.

He had been married while he was still a forester and had two children. He loved them dearly. When he found that his wife beat them he told her: "Don't do that again, or I'll kill you."

She shrugged and said, "You're away most of the time; I

66

have to keep your brats fed and washed. And if they're dis-obedient I beat them."

"I told you, don't. Because if you do . . ."

She did not believe him. A few weeks later when he paid another visit to his home he found that she had tied the little boy and the girl to the foot of the bed and was whipping them. So he shot her dead.

He took the children with him into the forest, where the wife of one of his men looked after them very well. For several years he took his women where he could find them, but just after the German invasion he fell in love with a Jewish girl from Bolechov. He visited her regularly, though they could not get married. And when the various deportations and liquidations of Jews began he took her to the forest to live with him.

Some of this Yankel told me, some of it I found out later for myself. Stach Babij did not make any difference between people: whether they were Ukrainians, Poles, Jews, did not matter to him as long as they measured up to his standards and did what he told them to do.

Yankel was living in the ghetto and he and Martha had fallen in love. But though he lived in the ghetto, he seemed to be coming and going most of the time on various mysterious errands. I had met him only as Martha's lover, and I liked him; he must have decided to size me up before he talked to me, but in the end he did. He told me about Stach Babij and his group which was now beginning to recruit new members and was operating near Dolina, some twenty-five miles from Stryj.

I told him I wanted to join, for I was ready to do anything. But Yankel said it wasn't easy. Stach Babij would accept only these who could bring a gun or some other weapon with them and who knew how to handle arms. I soon found out that to buy a revolver would cost four or five thousand zlotys, and, as far as I was concerned, the price could have been a million; I certainly had no chance of getting that sort of money together. But I decided to get one no matter what I had to do to obtain it. In the end it proved easier than I expected. I spoke to Lackritz, my father's friend, about it and he became so enthu-siastic that he promised to find the money. (As the man run-ning the carpentry shop he had many opportunities of getting money, and he had some himself.) We held a little council of war, and it was agreed that I would be the first to join Stach

Babij, then I would return to fetch my father, Lackritz, and my sister.

A few days after my first meeting with Yankel I went to the ghetto and gave the money to Martha, so that she could pass it on to him. (Lackritz had provided enough to buy weapons for all four of us.) Again it took a few days before the guns were bought. Yankel sent me word that I should again come to the ghetto because he was now ready to take me to the forest.

I was filled with excitement because, for the first time after so many humiliations and miseries, I was going to have a chance to repay at least part of the wrongs we had suffered. I said goodbye to Father and Martha, promising them that I would come back very soon to fetch them. We agreed on a signal and a meeting-place; Lackritz was again covering up for my absence from the labour camp.

16

Yankel arrived one evening in the ghetto. There were seven of us, young Jews, all eager to join up with Stach Babij. Yankel had done the trip many times, knew every corner and every path, so we got out of the ghetto and into the forest without any difficulty. Our first stop, after moving along the forest trails, was Babijuska. There we waited for a shepherd called Slavko Kozak, who was the link between the ghetto and the partisans. He always grazed his herd close to the woods and had his regular times and places for meeting the partisans. We waited for several hours until he gave us the signal: a German patrol had just passed, and within two hours we were at Stach Babij's forest camp.

He came to look us over, and we felt a little uncomfortable under his scrutiny, for he was quite a frightening figure. But when he had inspected us (he seemed to be more interested in our guns than in our appearance) he grinned and said we would do. At that time he had some forty Jews and four Ukrainians in his band; by the time I left the partisans his force had increased to over three hundred.

He told us that we had to obey all his commands without questioning or hesitation. No-one was to leave the camp or the forest without his permission; we all had to stick to one of the three squads into which he divided us. He mixed the earlier arrivals with the new ones, so that they could teach us the ropes. We soon discovered that he was a formidable organizer and that he hated the Germans and Russians in equal measure, though just now he was "concentrating" on the Germans. He was known throughout the district—and feared. He could go into any village in broad daylight and demand food or anything and they would give it to him. He had already killed one Ukrainian who had tried to betray him, and that reduced the chance of any future treachery.

His main problem was arms, for we did not have enough and were especially short of ammunition. Shortly after I joined him he led ten of us into one of the villages where there was a Ukrainian policeman who was supposed to have a little private arsenal. We walked into his house and Stach Babij said, "Give us the guns or we'll shoot you." The policeman did not even argue or hesitate. He just showed us the cupboard where five carbines and a fair amount of ammunition were kept, and we carried them off.

Stach Babij took good care that we should be trained. We practised target-shooting and stalking. Once he got hold of a few grenades, showing us how to pull out the pin and how to throw them. Not that we had much time for such training, and because ammunition was precious everything had to be learned quickly. And we *were* pretty quick learners. Stach Babij was both canny and careful. Whenever somebody joined us he immediately moved our camp so that the newcomers could not act as guides for the Germans.

It was getting cold and we built some huts from the branches we cut; we also dug holes which we lined with grass. All these were well camouflaged and impossible to see unless you came right up against them. We also built some cooking pits from rocks, stones, and broken bricks. Food we always had in plenty, because the villagers brought us what we needed and we also did a bit of hunting on our own. It was a free-and-easy way of life, certainly less strenuous than working at the army labour camp, hammering those endless nails; we had a lot of laughs and felt that we were growing stronger every day, ready to take on the Germans.

17

When I had been six weeks in the forest I asked Stach Babij if I could fetch my family from Stryj.

"All right," he said, "but you must go alone. That way we'll only lose you if the Germans catch you and won't risk other lives. But take care of yourself—I'd rather have you back with us than killed. . . ."

I promised I would be careful and next night set out for Stryj. It was two o'clock in the morning when I came to the labour camp. I gave our signal and Father slipped out of the hut in which we had our bunks. He looked grim and harassed. Soon I knew why.

The Germans had liquidated the ghetto, though they had not yet done anything about the labour camp. However, many people had been hiding in the bunkers and cellars which had been prepared through the last two years and which honey-combed the place. Father did not know what had happened to Martha—it would have been suicide to go to the ghetto while the round-up was in progress—but I said I would go and see, and if she were alive I would get her out.

I soon found out that it was impossible for me to enter the ghetto openly or try to slip in at night. In the morning the Germans came to the labour camp and asked for volunteers "for transport work". I volunteered. What they called "transport work" was loading corpses on carts and pulling the carts to a cemetery just outside the ghetto.

With some others I started about ten o'clock in the morning. The SS men were searching the cellars and hide-out places systematically; they dragged the people outside and shot them on the spot. Bodies, stripped naked, were sprawled all over the place; one or two were still alive, though just barely. I managed to slip away for a few minutes between loading two carts, and I gave the signal, softly. To my relief and surprise I heard it repeated only a few feet from where I was standing. I found Martha hiding behind a partition in the tiny kitchen of the house she had shared with the four other girls. I had to think quickly, for she could neither stay there nor could I take her into the open.

"Listen," I told her, "we have maybe three minutes. You must do exactly as I tell you."

Her teeth were chattering, but she took hold of herself and nodded.

"Yankel . . ."

"He's all right. No time to talk about him now. Take off your dress and your shoes . . . quickly. . . ."

She did so; I rolled up her things and thrust the bundle under my overalls. I cut my arm and smeared some blood over her face and chest. "Close your eyes," I said. "Keep them closed whatever happens. Breathe very softly . . . let yourself go limp. . . ."

Again she followed my commands. I picked her up and let her hang over my shoulder. I looked through the window; there were no Germans close by. I stepped from the house and carried Martha down the narrow lane towards the cart I had left on the corner. On the way I bent down and picked up another body, this time a genuine corpse, a thin, elderly man, and carried both to the cart. Then I loaded them both on the bottom and piled four others on top. I took care that Martha could just breathe, near the tail of the cart. I started to pull it. An SS man, seeing me pass, shouted at me to hurry up. "There'll be lots more to bury, Jew," he added, "so don't hang about!"

I began to hurry as much as I could, pulling the cart over the stones and ruts. I got out of the ghetto, and half an hour later reached the cemetery, where large mass graves had been already dug which were filling up rapidly. I picked a tall grave-stone and stopped the cart near it. I bent down and whispered to Martha, "I'm going to unload the cart. When you can move, jump behind the gravestone and flatten yourself against it. I'll be back for you. . . ."

She didn't answer, but I had no time to worry about her having heard me or not. I unloaded the bodies on the edge of the nearest grave, where five others from the labour camp were pulling and dragging them into the hole; then I hurried back to the stone. Martha was there, white as a sheet. When she saw me she tried to smile and I knew she would be all right. We moved quickly away from the gravestone into a slight hollow and from there made our way to the back gate of the cemetery.

71

We hid for the rest of the day in a half-ruined chapel, and I wanted to set out at once for the forest as soon as darkness fell. But I found that Martha was hardly able to walk. It was the delayed reaction to that journey on the cart, under the corpses. She said, "Leave me, Emil. Go on, I'll be all right." But I couldn't do that. I forced her to get up and took her to the labour camp, where I hid her in one of the store-rooms. Then went to see Father and told him what had happened.

"Let's get away now!" I pleaded. "All three of us. The Germans might start liquidating the camp tomorrow. . . ."

"I can't," he said. "You take Martha—"

"Why not?"

"Lackritz wants to come with us and he can't leave for a day or two. Take Martha and I'll follow you as soon as possible."

I argued with him for a while, but he was my father and I couldn't tell him how wrong I thought he was. I went back to Martha and found her in a much better condition, though still weak. One of the men had given her a little vodka and she had tidied herself—I had given her back her dress and shoes. She said she was willing to try the journey now. So we set out.

It took us four days, for she was much weaker than I thought and once or twice we had to dodge German patrols, making wide detours so as not to lead them to the partisan camp. When we got there Yankel was the first to see us. He and Martha had quite a reunion, as if neither had believed that he or she would see the other again.

I found a new group of Jews from Bolechov in the camp. There was a Dr Diamant, a very useful addition, for until then we had no medical men in our group; an engineer called Meter; a whole family called Begleiter; and several others. The older people were detailed to forage for food; they regularly went into the villages to collect the provisions which Stach Babij's Ukrainians and others had gathered for us. For every fighting member of the detachment we had two or three who did other chores. And most of our activities were nocturnal.

A few days later I decided to go back to Stryj and fetch Father before it was too late. I arrived at the labour camp on a Thursday; but even now Father refused to leave, saying that Lackritz and some other friends were not yet ready. I pleaded with him, but it was no use. Much against my better judgment,

I agreed to wait until Saturday. Father kept on saying that the Germans needed us, the winter was near, and they had to have more huts and barracks, that they would not deprive themselves of such a cheap labour force.

On Saturday I said I wasn't going to wait any longer; we must leave at once. He said if we had waited until now and nothing happened, let's wait till Sunday: there were fewer guards around and it would be easier to get away.

"But I have got in and out without any difficulty six times," I told him. "For pity's sake, Father, can't you understand?"

"Don't speak to me in that tone of voice! I am your father and I know what I am doing."

I was so angry I almost left him, but, of course, I couldn't. So we waited. Every hour or so I asked him whether he had changed his mind, but he was talking to Lackritz, then went off to collect some debt . . . and then, Saturday evening, the whole labour camp was surrounded. It was no use reproaching Father, that wouldn't have helped, but I swore that in the future I would never listen to him. Not that it looked as if there would be a future at all; I reconnoitred the whole place and everywhere the Ukrainians and the SS men were guarding the camp, with dogs and machine-guns. Soon they started to round up people. We could not hide; they went from barrack to barrack, from hut to hut. Finally they came to us and lined us up. I was standing next to Father and said, "Listen, please, and do what I tell you. No argument this time."

He just nodded; I suppose he was too ashamed to speak and I certainly did not want any apologies or explanations.

"They're going to march us through the town. I have a revolver and a hand-grenade hidden on me. When we get to the first cross-street you fire the revolver and we will make a run for it. . . ."

"All right, Emil," he said, very meekly. "We'll do that."

The Germans told us that we would only be transferred to another camp, though I knew better. We had to surrender all our tools and documents. They lined us up four abreast. In front of us were four young boys and when they heard me whispering to Father one of them turned and said, "We're going with you!" I couldn't argue, and I thought maybe if we were a bigger group we had a better chance—at least some of us would make it.

But first we had to wait. It wasn't until six o'clock in the

73

morning that the first group was taken away. They were guarded by SS men on all four sides, armed with automatic pistols, who escorted them to the Stryj prison. An hour later the same Germans and Ukrainians came back to collect the second group, mostly women. It was about nine o'clock before our turn came; we were the last group. We were told to cross our arms behind our backs and clasp our hands. When we reached the first corner I said to Father, "Now!" But he shook his head. "No, let's wait!" So we walked on. We reached the second corner and a German military car just drove by, so that was a chance we missed again. I thought that maybe Father couldn't get the gun out of his pocket because his hands were clasped. We walked on, with our escort spaced out along the long, straggling column. People were watching us from behind closed shutters, peeping round corners. We were already in the centre of the town, close to the prison. Only a few yards separated us from the main gate, then an SS man shouted, "Keep right!"

At this moment Father fired his gun—he must have managed somehow to get it out—and I threw the hand-grenade, though it did not explode. The Germans and the Ukrainians, thinking that it was a partisan attack, threw themselves on the ground. Father and I and a few others began to run; not in the same direction, though we had agreed where we would meet if any of us got away. The Germans and Ukrainians were now scrambling to their feet, but a good two minutes passed before they started to fire. Maybe they hesitated because there were many people around and they were afraid they would hit somebody from their own side. But pretty soon they set out in pursuit and I drew them after me, showing myself clearly; then I jumped a few fences, ran into a courtyard, then again into a street. I realized, however, that I was once more in the main street, so I rushed back, climbed a couple of roofs, and finally slipped into a woodshed. Here I noticed a large basket and crawled under it.

After a while several others burst into the shed and among them I recognized Srulek Horowitz, whom I could just see through the slits in the basket. Before long a lot of Ukrainians and Germans came into the shed, starting to beat the people, who screamed and wailed, then dragged them out. I saw that Srulek had slipped behind the door and stood there, rigid, waiting. Behind the basket there was a large crib with some corn.

I didn't want to alarm Srulek, so I kept silent. We both waited. About an hour passed, then suddenly I heard the barking of dogs. This was the end, I thought, and I pushed my shirt-tail into my mouth so that I shouldn't pant or breathe too loudly. Then the door opened, the dog rushed in, and jumped on Srulek. Soon the Germans followed, hitting, whipping, dragging him out while he cried, "I'm still young; have pity, I'm still so young!"

I waited. The dog was still sniffing around; then it lifted its hind leg and did its business against the crib. After that it left. I was alone now, but I couldn't move. I was bathed in sweat. My plan was to try to get to Sofia Miron, who was Srulek's sweetheart, a Polish girl, not a Jewess. If I could reach her she would help, I was sure.

After a while an old woman came into the woodshed, and as she moved to the crib she kicked the basket, which fell over. There I was, without cover!

"Jesus-Maria!" she cried. "A Jew!"

I clapped my hand over her mouth, pushed her into the crib —she fell deep into it; it would take her a minute or two to get out in her voluminous skirts—and ran. When I had crossed the yard I stepped into the street and, though the cold sweat ran in rivulets down my back, forced myself to walk slowly, calmly to the corner. Here I saw three Ukrainians, who were discussing the escape of the Jews right outside the prison. They were so excited and intent on their discussion that they did not even look at me. I continued in the direction of the labour camp and the sawmill. On the way I noticed a horse-cart driven by a Pole I knew who did some cartage for the mill. Without asking him, I jumped up and said, "Don't talk, let's go to the sawmill!"

He drove at a steady pace, but without forcing it. Just outside the labour camp I jumped off and managed to get through the barbed wire and into our underground hiding-place. Here we had built up some wooden posts and beams which camouflaged it well, and there were two entrances and exits which we had prepared with Father for emergencies. For a long time I sat there, listening to every sound. It was very quiet; I could hear my heart pounding and then gradually slowing down to a calmer beat. I thought that the hunt must be over, or at least that they would not think that anybody would double back to the place where the round-up had started. So I made myself a

75

little more presentable and went into the office where Sofia Miron worked.

She had already heard about the escape and the chase and asked me at once about Srulek Horowitz. I told her what had happened.

"Go back to your hide-out," she said, "and wait for me. I must go and see what I can do for Srulek. I must try to save him."

I did as she asked. Later she came back; she was very distressed, but not without hope. She had friends in the prison and had discovered that though they had beaten Horowitz badly, he was alive and in a part of the prison from which it might be possible to get out. She asked me what I wanted. I asked her for bread, cigarettes, and a worker's pass made out in the name of Emil Brikowski, driver. She came back in the evening and told me that perhaps during the night she might get Srulek out; she brought me all I had asked for, even a sheepskin coat, and wanted to give me money. Srulek kept his savings in her room. I did not take the money, but asked her to let my father know in case he turned up at the sawmill and tell him to make for the forest. I gave her the address of the shepherd in Babijuska who would bring him to Stach Babij's camp.

Sofia was quite a girl. Though she did not succeed that night, two days later she managed to smuggle Srulek from the Stryj jail; I met him again in Hungary.

I had a good night's rest and next morning, having said goodbye to Sofia, I left the sawmill and started towards the bridge across the Bistrzyca. As I had a pass with the official stamp, a pass that would stand up to all but the most severe scrutiny, I thought I would join a group of Poles who crossed the bridge every day to work in the near-by woods.

As I approached the bridge I noticed a Ukrainian policeman. At the same moment a man came out of one of the houses near the bridge, carrying a loaf of bread and a bottle of milk. He was barefoot and walked slowly, limping a little. He went up to the policeman and asked for a light, holding up his cigarette. My heart skipped a beat as I recognized him. It was Father. Without giving any sign, I passed him. He had lit his cigarette, thanked the policeman courteously, then sauntered on. I slowed down a little so that he could catch up with me. "Don't stop," he whispered. "We're going on!"

We crossed the bridge with the group of Poles, then turned into a field and crawled into a thicket of bushes. There I asked him what on earth he had been up to when I noticed him just now. He said that when he saw the policeman he became so confused with fear that he felt he just *had* to have a smoke, and didn't even realize what he was doing when he asked for a light.

When we separated outside the prison, he explained, he and the others made for the outskirts of the town. He didn't know the way; he and the eight others who were with him were chased by the Germans and lost their shoes scrambling over rough ground. They reached a small wood, but at noon had to leave it because some Ukrainians arrived. They ran and dodged pursuit until the evening. Then they decided to double back into the town, where it was less likely they would be hunted than in the open. Father found shelter with a farmer whose small house was close to the bridge. When he walked out in the morning the farmer gave him the loaf and the milk, which was helpful because, he thought, the police would believe that he lived there.

He asked me how I had fared and I told him about Srulek and Sofia. The others, it seemed, had either been caught or were hiding in the woods on the other side of the river. We waited until evening in that rather damp clump of bushes, then moved on towards Morszyn. It was a dark, moonless night and on the way we sank up to our waists in a swamp when we were trying to cross a small river. It was with great difficulty that we dragged ourselves free, though luckily it wasn't quicksand. We decided to stick to the high road and make a run for it if we were spotted. We were close to the railway track when suddenly a spotlight glared behind us. We ran as fast as we could, dropping to the ground whenever the spotlight swung in our direction. We were certain that they were still hunting us. Luckily we were not caught in the spotlight. We walked on towards Bolechov; in the distance we saw many motor-cycles, army vehicles, and command cars. The Germans were out in force.

Some time after midnight we came to a crossroads where a small house stood. We decided to take a rest in some near-by underbrush and go on in the morning. We kept an eye on the little house. Early in the morning two motor-cycles stopped outside, followed by a scout-car. The Germans knocked on the door and demanded, "Have you seen two people in brown overalls?"

A sleepy old man replied, "No, no, we've been asleep, we saw nobody."

This made it clear enough that they were looking for us and that we had to move fast before the patrols caught up with us. In the dim morning light we again followed the highway to the second bridge which led to Bolechov. We decided that if we were stopped we would say that our car had broken down, that Father was a driver, and that I was his mate, because the paper which Sofia Miron had forged for me said so.

We were very close to the bridge when we noticed that it was guarded by soldiers of the Vlassov Army, the Russian quislings the Germans had recruited. It was too late to turn back, they had seen us, so we walked on, and naturally we were stopped. We produced our pass and told the sergeant in charge that our car had got stuck in the swamp and that we were going to Bolechov to fetch some help to get it out again. The sergeant looked closely at the pass, but I noticed that he held it upside down. He obviously couldn't read German, and after a while he decided that he'd better let us go, for Sofia had added a very impressive stamp.

In the evening we got to Babijuska, and before long we met the shepherd who was the link with the partisans. He told us where we would find Stach Babij, and next morning we reached the camp. Within a few minutes we found Martha and Yankel, who were now sharing a hut. She had become quite an experienced and hardened partisan girl, but when she saw us she burst into very feminine tears. She hadn't expected to see us alive, for the news of the complete liquidation of the Stryj labour camp had already reached the forest.

Stach Babij was quite pleased to see us, too, for he needed every man he could recruit. We told him that we had been constantly followed by the German patrols, but Stach Babij said that it wasn't us they were looking for, but the first Russian parachutists who had dropped in the district. Some of them had been seen about ten miles from the camp. The Germans were apparently searching the edge of the forest in a wide arc, but did not come into the forest itself. They sent some Ukrainians and Vlassovists to deal with us and the parachutists, but even they did not penetrate very deeply. The Germans shelled and bombed the woods, but that didn't do very much damage except to the trees and the stray deer or hare.

By now it was the end of October. Kiev had fallen and the Russians had gone over to the offensive. The task of the parachutists was to cut the main railway-line to the hinterland and other lines that served the German retreat. Stach Babij decided to help them. He divided us into three groups. Father and I were in the one that was to operate around Krzywa, consisting of about forty men; Martha and Yankel were in the second, which, with a third one, was concentrated around Ludwikowska and Wygoda. The groups were separated by about five miles of forest. We began to operate systematically, first to gather food and clothing for the winter, ransacking the villages whenever necessary. These raids were made every second or third night. We also began to build bark huts which provided quite good cover against the cold and damp. Every hut held two or three partisans; I shared one with my father and Martha and Yankel had their own. We changed our camp very often and before long made our first contact with the parachutists, though it was unplanned and almost ended in a fight.

One day ten of us went on patrol. We noticed four armed men and surrounded them in a large circle. They called to us, saying they were partisans themselves, on our side. We decided to make sure, so we sent one man into the nearest clearing and they detached one of their group. It turned out that they were Russian parachutists who had been wandering around in the forest for two weeks, seeking to establish proper liaison with us. They showed us a portable radio-transmitter which worked on batteries, but could also be recharged by working a handstarter. As we were more numerous and the radio looked genuine enough, we took them to Stach Babij, who welcomed them and gave them a good deal of useful information. He also told the Russians about a Nationalist Ukrainian partisan movement called Bulbovcy whom one of our groups had met. They had told us that now we all had the same enemy, the Germans; but if the Russians arrived and we made common cause with them they would turn against us because they hated both Nazis and Communists alike. Luckily for us and for the first small Russian detachment, the Germans wiped out the Bulbovcy in a swift, concentrated attack.

In the meantime another four hundred Russian parachutists landed near Woldzirz, and now we started the first serious

79

operations against the Germans. In the beginning we had simply acted as guides because we knew the lie of the land so well. (The Russians had maps, but these were not entirely reliable.) Our relations were not particularly cordial; they were determined by the simple wish to survive. We certainly did not bother about politics; none of us had time to discuss Marxism or the future of the world.

Early in November one of our scouts brought the news that a German detachment had arrived near the forest. We were given the orders to attack. We started off, and the Russian parachutists attacked from the rear. We killed about half of the Germans and the others fled. We got some extra weapons from the dead, and above all boots, which we needed badly. A little later we blew up the Bolechov-Daline line in several places. In retaliation the Germans sent a large group of Ukrainians and Vlassovists on a "search-and-destroy" mission into the forest. We immediately sent word to the Russians. Generally speaking, the parachutists kept deep in the forest and we had contact with them only when they needed some help or when we had some important intelligence for them. Stach Babij gave us orders to leave our camp at once and move into the forest. We were divided into three units in order to attack the invaders from three sides. Fourteen men, among them myself, were picked to guide the Russians to Krzywa, where the Vlassovists had their headquarters. The Russians were equipped with light machine-guns; we only had some revolvers and a few, mostly old, rifles. During the night we surrounded the Vlassovist camp in Krzywa and early in the morning opened fire from three sides. The Vlassovists had only one way to escape, through a narrow ravine leading into the Carpathians. But the Russians had stationed several machine-guns at the far end of the ravine, and all the Vlassovists were mowed down. It was my real baptism of fire, and though I had no shoes (I hadn't been able to get a pair that fitted me from the dead Germans), I felt twice as alive as I had during the long months while I was on the run, from ghetto to the forest, from the forest to the labour camp, always on the move, but now no longer a hunted animal.

After the Krzywa battle (more like a massacre than a fight) we moved some twenty miles deeper into the forest. Twelve days later the Germans attacked a group of Jewish families who were hiding near Woldzirz. This camp contained only some older people, unfit to fight or make long marches, who had come to the forest simply to save their lives. The Nazis killed more than a hundred and forty of them; a few managed to escape and reach our camp. We found three survivors, all wounded, on the spot, but one died as we attempted to carry him to safety.

We moved camp again; nine days after the massacre of the defenceless old folk we heard that the Germans had sealed off the whole forest, blocked all paths and crossings. There were planes flying over us on long reconnaissance patrols. Though it was now bitterly cold, with deep snow, we did not light any fires and, in order to mislead the enemy, we went back to our former encampment. I shared one of our primitive huts with Father; Martha was in another group, about a mile and a half from us.

The concentrated attack came on November 29th, 1943. Our advance guard must have fallen asleep or something—we never found out what. But we were between two mountains and the Germans advanced from behind and opened fire on us, using big-calibre guns and machine-guns. We jumped up and took cover behind a tree. I stood next to my father when he was hit by a whole salvo—seven machine-gun bullets, which pierced him from knee to head. The Germans were firing from above us and he was killed instantly.

I climbed the tree and swung to another, higher one. There I sat, clinging to the topmost fork, until midday. I was out of the range of the German guns, though I did not know how long my precarious perch would hold out. But then the firing stopped. I waited another hour, then climbed down and found Father in a pool of blood, which was already frozen. I dug a shallow grave with my bare hands and buried him the best I could. There was no time for anything else, and I prayed for him while I was digging, silently, and biting on the thought that of my entire family only Martha and I were now alive.

I made my way to the bivouac where Yankel and my sister were. I did not tell Martha that our father was dead; I only said that there had been a short fight and that he had moved on with the others. But later Yankel and I went back where my group had been attacked. We found that twenty-two men had been killed and two were badly wounded. We wanted to carry them with us, but Dr Diamant, the Bolechov doctor who examined them, said that it would be useless: they could not live long and would only slow us down. It was a question of choosing between those two and the survivors. In the end Dr Diamant gave them a cyanide capsule each, which put them out of their misery.

On the same day the Vlassovists attacked the Russian parachutists' camp. The Russians fled in total panic; they were surrounded and outnumbered. It was a terrible disaster both for them and for us. Before the general attack was over only four of the Russians remained alive, and of my own group of fifty, five had survived—Begleiter and his wife, Hornik, Lustig, and I.

Somehow we made our way to the group of Yankel and Martha. On the way Lustig told me about an uncle he had in Carpatho-Ruthenia, which was then part of Hungary. The uncle lived in a little town called Huszt, not far from the Polish-Hungarian frontier. We knew that Hungary was still more or less independent, and had even heard rumours that Admiral Horthy was trying to sign a separate peace. True, Lustig had attempted to cross once before in 1942 and some Hungarian Jews had handed him, his brother, and his mother over to the German frontier police, who were working hand in hand with the dreaded Hungarian gendarmes, the *csendörs*. It was a desperate step to take, but we had no choice. We had lost contact with the Russians, for our group was on the other side of the mountain, and even if we had joined them we wouldn't have lasted long. The Germans were now combing the forest, covering every square yard. At least Hungary offered a fifty-fifty chance, perhaps even better odds.

I picked people who would stand up to the long and difficult journey. Lustig, Hornik, Begleiter, Yankel, and Martha were, of course, among them. So that we should have at least a little food, that night we raided a small Ukrainian village, took some bread and potatoes, and slipped away before the alarm could be raised.

We waited two days until snow started to fall, so that it would cover our tracks, and then, on December 5th, we set out, a motley, ragged group of twenty-four. I had no shoes; I wore only trousers, a shirt, and an old coat which had a huge hole burned in it. The others were clad similarly, except for Martha, who somehow managed to keep neat and warm.

It took us nine days to reach the frontier, for again and again we had to halt and wait for a new snowfall that would hide our tracks. Lustig gave us his uncle's address, which we all had to learn by heart—No. 10 Kraszna Street in Huszt—in case we got separated. We knew that there was a river on the road to Wyszkow and that we had to walk along its banks to reach Huszt. We approached the frontier and found barbed wire, the *concertinas*, as we called them, and on top of the mountain ridge there were the German frontier police. We decided to make a detour to avoid their look-out post, but stumbled over the trip-wire hidden under the snow which set off the alarm. The sirens began to howl. We turned and fled, but the Germans came hurtling down on skis, firing blindly, with dogs bounding at their sides. We fired back and then turned towards the near-by forest. One of the dogs was faster than the others, overtook us, and fastened its teeth in Jossek's leg. I shot it with my gun, but even in death it held on to Jossek's flesh, and as he tried to run, dragging it along, he fell and could not get up again before the Germans were upon him. We lost two others in that fight, a girl and a man; but luckily the Germans could not move fast enough in the woods, with the dense undergrowth. Running downhill, we managed to get away from them. We knew that the frontier passed along the highest ridge in that neighbour-hood, and once we had crossed it we were on Hungarian soil.

We moved on for two hours, as fast as we could, which wasn't very fast, for we were pretty near the end of our strength. My feet were frozen and swollen. We had had very little to eat during the past nine days, for what few provisions we could scrounge were soon gone. We gathered the bread-crumbs some of us had in our pockets, put them into a pot which we had filled with snow, and then made a kind of soup. We called it "pocket-soup", and that was our only nourishment. We slept under the trees, on the bare ground, wrapped in rags. Some-times we lit fires to rid us of the lice that had infested us.

The day after our battle with the frontier guards we reached the first settlement on the Hungarian side. The main group stayed in the woods, keeping a watch, while Martha, Yankel, and two other boys went into the nearest house to get some-thing to eat. We knew it was a risk, but we had no choice. The house was some five or six hundred yards away and we could keep it under observation, though we saw only the back of it—the yard and some sheds.

After about an hour Yankel came back and said that this was a Ukrainian settlement and that they had no food, but

83

promised to bake us some bread if we waited a little. We were hungry enough to agree, even though it was not very safe to remain in such an exposed place. Yankel said Martha was resting and the two boys were staying with her. Yankel went back to join them and we waited. After a while we saw a Ukrainian peasant woman drive a cow through the gate of the backyard, away from the house. We found this most suspicious. She was singing and we couldn't understand why she should be driving that cow through the deep snow, and if they had a cow, why hadn't they at least given us some milk? But there was nothing we could do and we were by then so dazed with the cold and hunger that we could barely think straight.

Another hour passed, then we heard sleigh-bells. It was a strange, incongruously pretty sound in the middle of our misery, just as the snow, the pine-trees, and the mountains were as beautiful as they were hostile. The sleigh was filled with German frontier guards. As we watched, helpless and aghast, we heard several shots being fired from inside the house. Yankel, Martha, and the boys were obviously firing at the Germans. Then came a whole series of shots and a machine-gun began to fire. I wanted to rush down, but Begleiter and another man held me back by force, sitting on me as I struggled and writhed. By the time they let me go the Germans had driven away. There was silence. We still waited. After another hour or so the Ukrainian woman returned, without the cow. She wasn't singing now.

I told the others that I wouldn't wait any longer. It was getting dark and we went into the settlement. Within the house we found the Ukrainian woman and two men. We asked them where our people were and they replied that they hadn't been in their house.

I was past endurance by then and I began to slap the woman. She said that the four who had come into the house had later hidden in the barn, where there was some hay. But that was all she knew—she had gone out herself, she wasn't there. So we went to work on the two men; with them it took a little longer until they started to speak. They said that our people had begun to fire from the barn, and the Germans returned the fire. Then the frontier guards carried off the wounded on their sleigh. We knew that they were lying, that they had not been wounded but killed, and the corpses taken away.

I killed the two men and would have killed the woman, too,

except that the others stopped me. They held me tight, forcing my arms behind my back, and dragged me from that house which smelled of dung and death.

We marched all night, not daring to stop, trying to get away from the frontier district as far as we could. And as we stumbled through the snow and ice I thought of Yankel and Martha, who had been foolish and daring enough to make plans, to talk about children and a home, about peace and contentment when it was all over. I thought of how I had brought Martha out of the ghetto on the cart, under the pile of corpses, and how she had waited patiently outside the railway guard's house after we had jumped from the train. Now they were both dead and I was alone. I was nineteen. I did not want to die. I don't know why, but I wanted to live, to stand up and fight as long as there was breath in my body and the flame of hate in my heart.

18

We reached the river and walked uphill, in the direction of Huszt. We could think of little else but food and we did not talk, for if we had we would only have screamed at each other. We were very close to a complete breakdown.

It was early in the morning when we reached the little village of Toronyevo, already well within Hungary. We saw lamplight in the low, thatched houses. I felt I had to do something, to court danger, even to provoke it, so I told the others to wait while I went into the village and asked for the shortest way to Huszt. Lustig warned me not to have anything to do with Jews, for they were certain to turn us in—they were terrified of the Hungarian gendarmes.

I left the rest of our group on the mountain-slope and knocked on the door of the first house. A Hungarian peasant opened the door. He spoke Ukrainian. I told him I was a Pole and that there were several others with me, that we had escaped from our country and were looking for work. He said he had no work himself, but there were some larger farms in and around the village which certainly could use some help. I asked him whether he could spare any food. He gave me a loaf of bread and a fair-sized piece of raw bacon—a princely gift indeed. I thanked him and already turned to go when he called me back and changed the black bread he had given me for another loaf of rye. He explained that if I were caught by the gendarmes the black bread, which was part of the regular ration, would betray *him*: they would know I had got it from a local farmer. And he warned me to keep out of the gendarmes' sight, I looked so disreputable and suspicious. And he warned me especially *not* to go into one particular house where a Jewish family lived who were certain to denounce me.

I took the bread and the bacon and hurried up to the hill where the others were waiting. I gave it to Lustig to distribute, so that everybody should have at least a bite (there were still seventeen of us left), then I returned to the village. I went straight to the Jewish house, defying the double warning. Something drew me there almost irresistibly. It was Friday and through the window I saw a woman who was kneading a *chale,* the Sabbath twist. It was so unexpected, almost shattering, for, of course, it reminded me of my mother and our own Sabbaths in Tarnow. I knocked on the door and someone called out, "Who's there?" in Ukrainian.

"A Jew," I replied in Hebrew.

A moment later a well-dressed young man stepped from the house. I told him I wanted to go to Huszt.

"All right," he said, "give me a bit of gold and I'll take you."

I had no gold, but I would have promised him anything. "Let's go," I said.

He replied that he would have to get dressed first, put on proper warm clothes. But he was already dressed in felt boots and a heavy coat. And the experience of the day before with the Ukrainians had taught me to be doubly suspicious and cautious. I took out my gun and pointed it at him.

"*Now,*" I said. "Start moving . . ."

He looked at me and saw that I meant it. I forced him to climb the hill, and found the others finishing the last crumbs of the food I had brought, but they had saved a portion for me. The young man said, "I can't take you to Huszt, it's almost twenty-five miles away, but I'll take you to Majdanka, that's only three miles from here and there are several Jewish families living there. We're all alone in Toronyevo and we can't do much for you."

We watched him all the time, but he made no attempt to run

86

away and took us to Majdanka, a village on the river-bank which was still quite close to the frontier. He led us to the synagogue, and there we were warmly welcomed by the small local Jewish community. As for our guide, when he demanded the gold, we told him that he would have to wait, and if he insisted he would get a beating. He went off, grumbling, and we never saw him again.

In Majdanka we met the first Jews who were in touch with the Waad Hahacala, the Rescue Committee, whose headquarters were in Budapest, with Joel Brand in charge. There was a local Jewish Council, and the Hagana brigade, charged with passing the escaped Polish and other Jews from Huszt to Budapest, also had its local representative. The organization worked under great pressure and against heart-breaking odds, but it seemed to be efficient enough. They immediately sent word to Budapest, and while we were waiting for forged papers and transport we were divided up among various families. Lustig and I found reasonably comfortable quarters in the attic of an old Jew. We still had to be extremely cautious because Majdanka was regularly raided by the frontier guards and the Hungarian gendarmes; many Polish refugees, especially Jews, were tortured and executed if they were caught. We had another problem: we had to get used to eating again. Lustig became quite ill when he made too hearty a meal and I had some trouble too, though I tried to control my appetite.

One night about half-past eleven our host climbed up to the attic and said, *"Chaver*, you'd better start running—the Gestapo is coming!"

"But where shall we go?" I asked.

"Follow the river to Soimi . . . if you get across the bridge you'll be safe."

We slipped from the house and reached the bridge about an hour later. We wanted to cross it when a Hungarian soldier started to shout at us:

"Allj! Allj!"

We didn't understand him and thought it rather funny that he should cry "Ay! Ay!"—at least that's how it sounded to us. Then he added something like *"Vissza! Vissza!"* This again was like the word "visa", though why he should ask for that we don't know. We still walked on, and it wasn't until he struck out at us with his rifle that we realized we couldn't go on. We went into the nearest house, which was luckily a Jewish one.

They hid us and explained that we were indeed lucky that the soldier, who must have been a recent recruit, did not call the border police. *"Allj!"* really meant *"Stop!"* and *"Vissza!"* was the Hungarian for *"Back!"*—the first two Magyar words we learned.

We were now separated from our group and in a difficult situation. In the meantime the Budapest Rescue Committee had made a deal with some Germans, civilians, who were transporting timber from Northern Hungary to the capital. They were to carry our group hidden under their load to Huszt. Their price was high, more than two thousand dollars, and had to be paid in cash and in advance; but apparently the Committee did not lack funds. And it had a highly efficient communication system, for the lorries arrived promptly at Majdanka. It was dusk and they were about to get under the carefully arranged timber when Hornik noticed that Lustig and I were missing. He told the others who were already on the lorries to get off and start looking for us. Some protested, saying that the transport had cost so many dollars, that every moment's delay might bring the German border guards or the Hungarian gendarmes upon them, that it was better to leave.

"And what about Lustig and Brigg?" Hornik demanded angrily. "Isn't their life worth anything?"

He insisted that they should wait while he ran to our host's house. The old Jew told him that he had roused us in the night and that we had gone on to Soimi. The German drivers promised that they would pick us up in Soimi, which was on the way to Huszt. But the lorries did not even stop in the village and there was nothing Hornik could do—he was by then hidden under the timber and didn't even see where they were going. It was only in Huszt that he discovered what had happened. He gave us up for lost.

19

But we were quite comfortable in the little riverside house. A few days passed and then the daughter of the family that had hidden us gathered a group of girls from the village. Lustig and I had tried to make ourselves as presentable as possible, and, surrounded by the girls, we walked to the bridge. We were told to say, "*Igen! Igen!*" ("Yes! Yes!") from time to time, to laugh and pretend to tease the girls. The girls made much of the sentry, telling him jokes, offering him candy. It seemed like a gay Christmas party and he let us pass without asking for any papers or even giving us a second look.

When we got to the other side we were again lodged with a Jewish family, and they sent a message to the Rescue Committee. A few days later a car arrived to take us to Huszt. We were happy and relieved, but our joy was somewhat premature. The car broke down and we had to hide again. We spent the whole night in the synagogue of Wolov, hiding under the pews. When some Jews arrived in the morning we crawled out and they surrounded us, asking innumerable questions, to most of which we had to return very unhappy answers. The news of our presence spread, more and more people came to see us, and they all brought us food, so that we began to feel as if we were the principal guests at some banquet.

Lustig asked about his uncle in Huszt. One of the Wolov Jews was a friend of his and immediately went to telephone him. (A fairly simple thing like a telephone-call was a miracle to us. There were no telephones in the ghettoes or the labour camps—at least none we could use. And there were certainly none in the forest!) Within a few hours the uncle arrived (in a taxi!) and took us to his home in Huszt.

20

The first thing for which we asked in Huszt was a hot bath. It was something I had dreamt about for months and it seemed as unlikely a dream as the end of the war or the death of Hitler. But now Mrs Lustig filled a large tub with hot water. When I undressed they took my clothes and burned them, for they were crawling and swarming with lice—so thickly that there must have been a dozen for every thread and every strand of wool. Lustig's uncle gave us new clothes, and it was a wonderful feeling, after years of filth and raggedness, to be clean and neat again. My feet were still sore, but I was given some ointment and within a few days they were almost healed.

Here we met Hornik and the other members of our group and I heard how Hornik had tried to find us in Majdanka. We also heard about the Jewish organizations working in Hungary —the Hagana and the Hanoar Hazioni. Some were set up to save and aid the people who had managed to escape from the German-occupied territories. In spite of the severe anti-Jewish laws, Hungary was still a kind of refuge. We came now under the protection of the Hagana. Of course, the Polish section was headed by Polish Jews who already had the necessary contacts. Whenever someone got over the frontier their local man imme-diately telephoned Budapest and a representative travelled up from the capital, asking questions about where the new arrival came from, what he wanted, whether he was to be trusted.

Not long after we reached Huszt the necessary forged papers arrived and our group left by train for Budapest. There were no untoward incidents on the long journey and we started to discuss our plans. We wanted to join Tito's partisans if they were willing to accept us, but above all we wanted to get to Palestine.

In Budapest we were given some money—not too much, just enough to buy our meals, and we had considerable diffi-culty in finding a place to live. Our papers were only good for the journey and anyone living there illegally had to pay twice or three times the usual rates in a hotel or boarding-house. Partly because of this and partly because I wanted to move on as quickly as possible, I sought contact with the Hanoar Hazioni, the youth organization which I had joined as a child. I found a group of the Hanoar whose members all came from Sosnowitz and who lived in a tight little community, sharing all their resources, holding regular meetings. They put me through quite an inquisition, but when I told them about my life with the partisans and provided the necessary references they accepted me wholeheartedly. They suggested that I should join them, but now it was my turn to find out what their aims and activities were. They told me that they had five main goals which together constituted a sort of developing programme. They were doing their best to prepare the Hungarian Jewish youth for the time when the Germans would either occupy the country or turn it into a battlefield; they were busy forging "Aryan" identity documents for all the members of the group; they had already obtained some weapons and were training everybody in their use; they had established an initial contact

90

with the Yugoslav partisans through some Jewish Communist couriers who were able to move freely between Northern Yugoslavia and Hungary and hoped that before long we could in a body, join Tito's forces. Finally they aimed at the *Aliya Beth* (illegal immigration) to what they firmly believed would become the Jewish homeland.

All this was very much to my taste and I joined the group, which was living in a boarding-house in the heart of the city. Next day Tusia Herzberg (or, as she was known by her "Aryan" name, Jadwiga) took me to a department store and bought me a suit, a pair of shoes, and some other necessities. I shared a room at the boarding-house with two others. This was an entirely new life for me, and even my name changed, for I picked that of our Polish friend, Tomaszkiewicz, and only kept my given name to remember it better. My new friends and I all became Aryan Polish refugees with proper papers and identities, which gave us a fair amount of security, especially as the Germans had no direct power yet in Hungary.

In the meantime the group with which I had crossed into Hungary decided to go back into the woods, into illegality. It was impossible for them to find work and they were afraid of the regular raids of the Hungarian police, who were looking for Jews and Allied agents. They did not trust their new forged documents, or perhaps their nerves had suffered too much. They set up a community in the forest near Huszt. There, in March 1944, their hiding-place was betrayed by the local people. The Germans surrounded it and killed all who were in the underground shelter with hand-grenades. Six of them, however, happened to be out foraging for food, and they survived. Much later I met them in Israel and there they told me their stories: each of them had gone through a lifetime of adventure and suffering.

For us, too, the Hanoar Hazioni group, the situation became more and more difficult. Though officially we were Aryans, even the non-Jewish refugees were now forbidden to remain in Budapest, but had to move to smaller provincial towns. So we had to find a new shelter. We chose a small town called Mohács, south of the capital, on the Danube, near the famous battlefield where the Turks defeated the Hungarians in the early sixteenth century, ending the country's independence for three hundred years. It was close to the Yugoslav frontier and there were no other Jewish "underground" people living there. Our group had forty-two members, of whom twenty-eight young men and women moved to Mohács, while the rest remained in Budapest.

Our papers seemed quite all right, though we later discovered that the Pole who worked at the Hungarian police headquarters marked the documents of all those whom he suspected of being Jews with a special number. However, it was a considerable boon to have any papers at all, and the Rescue Committee had good relations with the Hungarian police, bribing them generously whenever it was necessary.

We all acquired new names. Jacob Rosenberg became Joseph Zelazo, Pinek Treiman became Boleslaw Dzido, Olek Gutman became Stanislaw Kolodziejczyk, Danka Firstenberg became Danuta Damalska, and Henryk Diamant became Mieczyslaw Starzewa—all good, solid Polish names. After a while the parents of some of our members also joined us in Mohács, all with proper Aryan documents and different names from those their children had chosen. We rented a few rooms in the houses of Jewish and Aryan families and tried to find work, for our money was getting short and the Rescue Committee had far too many burdens to carry.

I soon got a job with a locksmith, a Hungarian who spoke German, so that we had no difficulty in communicating. I began to learn Magyar and made a little progress, though my accent was atrocious. We made friends with a number of local families who later proved of great help to us. One of them consisted of a woman with five children whose husband had been called up for military service and who was in trouble when the usual time for pig-killing, an annual event in Hungary, arrived. I volunteered and did the "execution" perfectly, helping her also with the making of sausages and the curing of hams. She invited our whole group for a *disznótor*, the "pig's wake", which was a real feast. There was plenty of wine and the lady confessed to me that she had long suspected me of being a Jew, but now she was certain I must be a true-born Gentile because no Jew would have been able to do such a great job at the pork-butcher's craft!

I also found myself a girl. Her name was Genia Fuchs; she was Polish and a Jewess and lived with a peasant family on the outskirts of the near-by little town of Baja, also on the Danube. (Genia survived the war and the German occupation quite safely.) Though we were not supposed to leave Mohács without a special permit, I went to see her every week for a couple of days. She was slim and pretty and we were young enough to forget, at least for a few hours, all the danger and suffering of the past. I told her about Olga, and that brought her even closer to me. I begged her to come with us when we made our next move, for we had decided to join Tito's partisans as quickly as possible. The Hagana was already establishing regular contact with the nearest Yugoslav group; however, we needed arms. We tried to buy them, but could not find any in Mohács. In February I decided to go back to Soimi, where Lustig and I had hidden our revolvers and a few hand-grenades before we left for Huszt. I said nothing to any member of the group, as I wanted to be entirely responsible for any failure or trouble.

I boarded the boat in Mohács and had a pleasant trip up-river to Budapest. I planned to take the train from there to Soimi, but as I disembarked near the Houses of Parliament I ran into Danuta and Boleslaw, who were rather surprised to see me.

"What are you doing here?" Danuta asked. "Aren't you supposed to stay in Mohács?"

I told them about my plan for fetching the arms. Boleslaw took me by the shoulder and marched me round the corner, where he pulled me behind a hoarding. There he slapped my face hard and said, "You're not to do anything crazy, understand? What if you're caught?"

"That's my worry."

"Don't you think you're risking all our lives?" I tried to speak, but he slapped me again. "Keep quiet! Take the next boat back to Mohács! And don't ever let me catch you disobeying orders again!"

I couldn't understand why he was so angry, but Danuta explained that the police had searched our last quarters in Budapest, the boarding-house, and had found three revolvers in the room of one of the girls. Now they were looking for all the people who had been registered at the same address and who had left. So we needed extra caution lest the whole Hagana organization should be rounded up.

I realized that Boleslaw Dzido was right, even though I didn't very much like being slapped by him. He was three or four years older, so I swallowed my pride and went back to Mohács. But I still felt somehow naked and helpless without any weapons. We began to make cautious inquiries and found that some of the gipsies had arms to sell. I prepared a hiding-place under the windowsill of the room I shared with three other boys, on the ground floor, and arranged it so that if they were looking for something from the outside the stuff could be hidden on a ledge inside, and if they were searching inside the room it could be slid to the exterior part. The gipsies asked no questions; for money they would sell anything or anybody. Within a few weeks we had seven revolvers. We also studied Hebrew with Fela Fojk, a pretty girl who later married Pinek Treiman, or, aş his Aryan papers said, Boleslaw Dzido.

Apart from needing a permit to leave Mohács, we also had to report every Sunday to the local police station. Captain Albert, who was in charge, became quite friendly with us and we liked him very much. One day he told us, "There's another Pole living here, his name's Victor Janikowski, you'll meet him before long, I'm sure."

We were certain that this "Pole" must also be a Jew and found it somewhat strange that he didn't try to establish contact with us. He lived at the far end of the town and no-one among us had yet seen him. We sent a report to the Hagana in Buda- pest and they promised to look into the matter.

In the meantime we received the news about the first legal transport of Jews who were to be sent to Palestine via Switzer- land—a thousand people for whom the Rescue Committee had made arrangements with the Gestapo. Four places had been reserved for members of our group, all of them women. We also heard that our own organization had established certain links with Rumania and that those who managed to get there had a good chance of moving on to our final goal. Several members of the Hanoar Hazioni were already in Bucharest.

Ours was not the only Polish group which was working under the general direction of the Hagana Centre in Budapest. It was soon evident that they had started to organize their net- work long before we got to Hungary and in preparation for the worst—a complete German take-over of the country. We had ourselves recruited a number of young people to help us with forging documents and other things for which a know- ledge of the language was needed. Some of them we instructed in the use of arms—in particular one group in Balatonboglar, on the big lake. Not that all Hungarian Jews were ready to join the Hagana. Some of them (well, quite a number) said that in their country nothing could happen, nothing as bad as had happened in Poland. We did not try to argue with them, for they were set in their ways. But the younger people *did* listen to us, and a number joined and helped us, and thus a good many of our members managed to survive the terror that was soon to overwhelm Hungary. We had little or no contact with the Christian Polish refugees in Hungary; but among the Hungarians we met Siegfried Roth, who held a leading position in the organization and who now lives in London. There was still another group consisting of Jews from Transylvania. But all these were separate entities and we did not even communicate much with the Hanoar Hazioni members in other towns and villages, as we did not want to put anybody in jeopardy or wish to take unnecessary risks ourselves.

Before long we had no choice: the risks were thrust upon us. On March 19th, 1944, our landlord rushed into our room. He was almost incoherent as he began to shout: "Horthy . . . arrested . . . Germans everywhere . . . shooting people . . . arresting everybody . . . we wanted to get out of the war . . . but everywhere there're traitors . . . they won't let us . . ."

I waited until he calmed down, and then discovered that the Germans had decided to occupy Hungary, that a pro-Nazi government had been appointed, that Regent Horthy and his family were under arrest. I took the seven revolvers from their safe place and hid them under my coat. Then I called on the others in our group. We decided to distribute the guns among ourselves and to be even more careful than before.

For a while nothing seemed to happen: our life continued, our forged papers seemed to give us safety. But one day I met Janikowski outside the police station when he was just coming out. (I had seen him once before when one of the Hungarian girls pointed him out to me.) He turned and looked at me as I was measuring him up, and I knew at once that he was a Jew, though he was fair and had blue eyes. I walked up to him and asked him, in Yiddish, "Where are you from?"

He seemed startled and reluctant to speak; so I told him I was a Jew myself, though now I used the name Tomaszkiewicz. He said he was from Cracow.

"Why did you come to Hungary?"

"The same reason you came—I didn't want to stay in Poland any longer. I've been in Mohács for over a year. I keep out of trouble."

He nodded and walked away. I didn't see him for a few days, but one Sunday Genia came to visit me from Baja. I hadn't been to see her for a while and she was getting worried. We had a drink and were crossing the main street of Mohács when Janikowski came out of a shop and passed within a few yards. I felt Genia's hand on my arm, her fingers digging deep into my flesh. I turned to her; Janikowski had disappeared by then, and she was white as a sheet.

"What is it, Genia?" I asked. "What's the matter?"

She tried to speak, but couldn't. Then suddenly she went limp and I just caught her before she collapsed in a faint. I carried her to a near-by chemist's shop and got some smelling-salts. She recovered quickly enough and put her finger to her lips to warn me not to speak.

I took her home.

"That man . . . who came out of the shop . . . you saw him?"

"You mean Janikowski?"

"That's not his name."

"I know. He's a Jew like us; he's got false papers."

She shuddered. "His eyes . . . those blue eyes . . . I'll never forget them."

"What about them, Genia?"

"You know what he did? He got together a group in Cracow. I was one of them. Twenty people. He asked two thousand dollars apiece for taking us safely to Czechoslovakia and then to Hungary. He guided us to the frontier, where he handed us over to a Pole who was supposed to take us farther, but who led us straight into an ambush of the Gestapo and the frontier guards. We were all arrested, and those who resisted were killed on the spot. I was wounded and they left me for dead. Look . . ."

Genia had always refused to let me make love to her in daylight or with the lamp on. Now she pulled up her blouse. There was a long, jagged scar running down from her left armpit to her hip. It had faded, but it was still clearly marked.

"I got through . . . but those blue eyes . . . the eyes of the traitor . . . I'll never forget them."

Later I found out that five other people had survived from three different groups which Janikowski had also sold to the Gestapo. But no-one knew where he was, or even that he was in Hungary, until Genia and I saw him.

"It's all right, Genia," I told her. "He'll be punished. We'll deal with him—and soon."

But she was still so upset that she asked me to let her go back

96

to Baja and I put her on the train. As soon as she had gone I phoned Budapest and told them, in guarded terms, what I had discovered.

A couple of days later Dzido and two others from the Hagana headquarters in Budapest came down to see us. They had gathered a good deal more information about Janikowski. He was born in Stommik, near Cracow. He was an informer and *agent provocateur*, working with the Gestapo almost from the beginning, both in Cracow and in Dzialoszyce. He had free passes on the railways, could travel wherever he wanted. He worked hand-in-glove with a Jewish *Kapo* called Bialabzoda, a concentration camp guard who was later handed over by the Germans to Poland and hanged.

Janikowski organized a great many groups of Jews whom he promised to lead to Slovakia—for very high pay. Usually he took them only to the frontier, where the border police, notified in advance, awaited them. Janikowski was also "arrested" each time, but then released to continue his dirty work. However, by 1943 news of his activities had spread among the Jews in the ghettoes and he began to worry that he would be killed by the relatives of some of the people he had sold to the Gestapo. So he crossed into Hungary and settled down in Mohács. He had plenty of money and lived fairly quietly. But the Germans and the Hungarian Nazis naturally knew about his past and forced him to continue his treacherous activities. He was even serving the Hungarian Arrow Cross and the extreme Nazi Szalasi regime, providing the Gestapo and the Hungarian secret police with regular information.

Early in April Dzido and two other members of the Budapest group came to Mohács. They told us about the arrangements for our escape from Hungary. We had to get some forged police passes in order to be able to leave Mohács. They gave us detailed instructions and then left.

To get the passes was not an easy job. Luckily we had made friends with some Hungarian girls who came from the German-speaking villages in the neighbourhood. One of them became Olek's sweetheart. She had been a secretary and could type very well. Olek persuaded her to help us, which wasn't very difficult, because although she was of German origin she hated the Nazis. She took some old passes and copied them to perfection. Now we needed Captain Albert's signature. We had specimens of it on our own documents (he signed every time we reported

to the police station) and Wojcik could imitate it without difficulty. The hardest thing was to get hold of the official stamp,
which we couldn't forge. Fela Fojk volunteered to get it.

Next Sunday we went to the police station as usual. Fela was
the last in the line as we waited to have our identity-cards
stamped. While we chatted with Captain Albert she stole the
stamp from the desk. Nobody noticed it. Next day two of us
applied for a single pass to go to Budapest and returned the
stamp at the same time. It all went quite smoothly and we
reported to the Committee that we were ready to leave.

All of us in Mohács were burning to go; we were so close, we
felt, to reaching freedom, to starting on the first stage to our
Promised Land, that we lost all sense of reality. If you long for
something terribly hard, if you have thought about it for years
and years, when you are close to it, within arm's reach, so to
speak, you forget everything else. Just like being in love with
somebody and seeing nobody but that one person in a crowd
of a thousand people.

Then, just as we were making our final arrangements, Dzido,
Zelazo, and Janowski arrived from Budapest. They told us that
the Hagana Committee had tried Janikowski on the basis of all
the evidence they had collected—they had even gone to Baja
and talked to Genia, they had photographed him secretly and
spoken to the other survivors of the groups he had betrayed—
and had sentenced him to death. The three of them, they said,
had been assigned to carry out the sentence, while we were to
complete the travel plans. Our job was to send off the members
of our group in small "detachments", make sure that they had
everything they needed, cover up for them, and then, when they
were all gone, to leave ourselves. We were to travel via Pécs, an
old provincial capital not far from the Yugoslav border, to
Budapest. Apart from the five people chosen for this final
phase, no-one knew anything about the death sentence or the
further plans: they were all preoccupied with the final departure that was now so close.

But on April 22nd, 1944, Dzido received sudden orders from
Budapest. He and his two companions were called back to the
capital for some important mission: they did not tell us what
it was, and they left it to us to execute Janikowski.

We had no time to waste. The same evening we sent some of
the parents of the members of our group to Budapest. On April
24th another half-dozen left, and the same evening some more

98

went off. By now the majority were gone. Only nine of us remained in Mohács and we prepared our final task.

For a couple of weeks now Danuta Damalska had been meeting Janikowski, and leading him on quite skilfully. (It had been decided to ask her to do this because we wanted to get some more information out of him to send to the Hagana; we wanted to know particularly whether there were others engaged in the same filthy trade.)

Now Danuta sent him a note, inviting him to meet her on the river-bank in the evening. We arranged that Olek and I would hide behind a fisherman's hut and, when they passed by, shoot him. Then two other members of the group would join us to get rid of the body.

The first part of our plan worked well. It was just after eight o'clock when Janikowski and Danuta appeared on the foot-path. Olek stepped forward and barred their way. The girl moved to one side as Olek asked, "What did you do in Poland?"

That was the arranged signal for using our guns. But at the last moment we had to change our plan. It was a quiet evening and there were far too many fishing-boats on the river, some of them within a hundred yards or so. The shots would certainly have raised the alarm. So Olek hit Janikowski over the head with a knuckle-duster. He fell like a stunned ox. We tied his feet and hands and gagged him. He was still alive. Olek and I stabbed him several times with our switch-blade knives which we always carried. Then, with the other two, we lifted him and threw him in the Danube. Danuta still stood apart, on the spot where we had first accosted him.

We were not very practised assassins and this time we committed at least one fatal mistake. We forgot that the Danube was in flood and that the water along the banks was quite shallow. But we didn't have time to steal a boat and get into the middle of the river: there were too many fishermen about and someone would have been certain to see us throw a body into the water.

There were other mistakes. After we got rid of Janikowski we walked along with Danuta whistling some Hungarian airs, so as not to rouse the fishermen's suspicions. (At least we thought that would help; whether anybody who heard us could tell that we were not Magyars, I don't really know.) We went to Wojcik's room, where I changed my clothes because my

99

coat and trousers were spattered with blood. We hastened to destroy all papers so as to leave no trace behind. It was arranged that Wojcik would weight my clothes with stones and throw them into the river. I had changed into slacks and a pullover. But Wojcik, as I later found out, was too frightened to go back to the Danube. Instead he just rolled up the clothes and threw them on the roof of the next house. This was particularly unlucky because these were the clothes I had been wearing when I had my photograph taken for my documents. Nor did Wojcik tell us what he had done when he rejoined us. It is hard for me to blame him, though, for that was the first time he had seen death, violent death, so close and he was perhaps more excited, less his normal self, than the rest of us.

We waited until the morning; none of us slept. At 4.30 A.M. we walked to the bus-stop from which the bus was to leave for Pécs at 5. We got on the bus, but before it left the police arrived and started to check documents. Everybody had his or her papers, but I was afraid to show mine. So they told me to get off. Meanwhile the others left. I hoped that I could catch the next bus, which was due to leave four hours later, for not all buses were controlled by the police and it was unlikely that they would check papers again so soon after this.

As I waited I noticed a number of policemen and gendarmes all moving towards the river. Then some people who came back from the Danube stopped close by and began to talk about a body being found, the murderers being sought. (By then I knew Hungarian well enough to understand them.) I realized that I was in serious danger and that I had to warn the others, if at all possible. I started to walk, hoping to find some way of getting away, when I noticed a fine new bike leaning against a hedge. Without a moment's thought or hesitation I got on it and started to pedal as fast as I could. Pécs was less than twenty miles away and I covered the distance in about two hours. I left the bike on a corner and walked to the railway station, where I met my friends who had travelled on the early-morning bus.

We discovered that there was no train for Budapest until nine o'clock in the evening or 5 A.M. the next morning. I wanted to go back and pick up the bike; even though it was a considerable distance, I thought it would be better to get away from Pécs at once. However, Olek and the others started to argue that it would be madness to risk being picked up, that it would

100

take me a couple of days, so I gave up the idea. We decided that we would split into two groups, one to take the nine-o'clock train, the others the one next morning. It would be much less conspicuous if we did not travel as a large group. Again I agreed—and that was the third serious mistake we made.

We had plenty of time, so we went to a hotel, took some rooms, rested, and ate, then went back in the evening to the station. The first group, due to leave at 9 P.M., split up into smaller "detachments". I was in the first with Szerlok, Wojcik, Tobka, Giela. The girls all had guns hidden in their bras, and we were alert, ready for trouble. In order to avoid calling special attention to ourselves, it was decided that only two of us would go up to the ticket-office and ask for three tickets each. I was the first and I said in Hungarian, "Three second class to Pest, please."

"Keleti vagy Nyugati?" asked the clerk. (This meant "Western or Eastern Terminus?")

My Hungarian wasn't good enough to cope with the un-expected question, so I said, in German, "I don't understand."

The clerk shook his head and looked up. This must have been a signal, for suddenly two policemen appeared. I pro-duced my gun and was about to fire, but someone caught my hand from behind. It was a third policeman. They twisted my arms and led me away to the police station, which was in the same building. At the same time they must have started a check-up throughout the station, for soon other members of our group joined me. We were searched, but rather super-ficially: they did not find the guns which the girls had hidden. Then we waited. Altogether twelve of our group were arrested; the rest of them managed to get to Budapest by different routes. One even took a taxi.

We waited in the police station all night. In the morning they told us, "Get dressed, we're going", for they had taken away our shoes and jackets. They did not tell us where. We were handcuffed and shackled together in pairs, then a Black Maria came and took us to the central prison of Pécs.

101

21

A police captain was the first to receive us. He looked at us and screamed, *"Zsidók! Piszkos Zsidók!"* (Jews! Filthy Jews!")

Nobody said anything, except me. I thought it would be better to deny it. Not that it made any difference, he paid little or no attention to me. He made us walk down a steep flight of stairs. We found ourselves in a dark corridor, where they kept us waiting for a while. I was worried about the guns which the two girls had on them. But I had no chance to talk to them, because soon a sergeant arrived and called us into an office, one by one. There they took our particulars (of course we gave the details as in our forged papers), then led us back to the corridor. When it was my turn and I came back I whispered to the girls to give me the guns. I had seen a sand-box in one of the corners, part of the usual air-raid-precautions equipment, and I managed to bury them deep under the surface.

The girls were taken into one cell, and four of us, Szerlok, Wojcik, the father of one of the other boys, and myself, were pushed into a large cell which had a lot of other prisoners already in it. There were about twenty of us all told, among others some Yugoslav partisans who had been dropped only a few days earlier.

It was about two o'clock at night when we were put into the cell. About six o'clock in the morning I heard two Hungarian warders talking outside the door. They said something about Polish partisans starting a fight, with guns and knives, at the station. Then I realized that our second group that was supposed to leave Pécs at five o'clock in the morning for Budapest had also been arrested.

An hour later they too were brought into our cell. Olek told me how they were also ambushed, though some of the first group had managed to get away, and two or three of the second as well. We began to talk to the Yugoslav partisans and found that we could communicate quite well with them. I asked them about any chances of escaping. They said that once a day they took the prisoners into the yard for exercise; that was the only possibility, though not a very promising one. But we decided to try, anyhow, and I thought that if they escorted us along the dark corridor I would have a chance to collect those two guns from the sand-box.

Our chance never came. About noon all the Poles were taken from the cell. We were again handcuffed in pairs, and six policemen guarded us closely as we left the prison and were taken to the station.

Except for the five of us, Olek, Szerlok, Danuta, Wojcik, and myself (for Starzow had managed to escape from the station the day before), nobody among us knew why we were being taken back to Mohács. (We had kept the Janikowski business from everybody else; these were our orders.) I was sitting next to Wojcik and whispered to him that I was going to try to escape, for I was certain that once we got to Mohács I was finished.

"But how are you going to do it?" Wojcik wanted to know.

I said I'd ask the policeman to take me to the lavatory, and when he removed the handcuffs (which he had to do, as we were shackled together in pairs) I would jump. After all, I had already done it a couple of times and had learned how to avoid hurting myself when I fell from a moving train.

"Don't do it, Emil," Wojcik began to plead with me. "It isn't certain why they're taking us back, maybe it's just to check our papers. You'd only put the others in danger. I can't believe that they've already found out about our share in Janikowski's death."

Wojcik was my friend and he could be very persuasive, so once again I gave in, much against my convictions. When we arrived in Mohács they took us straight to the police station. In the corridor we saw all the Hungarians with whom we had been lodging. They whispered to us that they had been questioned about when each of us left their houses.

We were summoned singly into Captain Albert's office. As I entered I saw at once my bloodstained suit. The Captain first asked my name, then told me to point out my landlord.

"Do you recognize these clothes?" the Captain asked.

"Yes, they're mine, but my friend Starzow borrowed them from me some weeks ago."

I said this because I knew that Starzow had managed to get away.

The Captain nodded. "Do you know a man called Janik-owski?" he asked.

"I met him once or twice," I said.

"Do you know he has been murdered?"

"No. When did it happen?"

But the Captain did not reply. "Take them away," he said, and we were all ushered into another bare room.

They lined us up against a wall, and a man came in, walking down the line, from one end to the other and then back again. He looked at us closely, but said nothing. Then two other men came in and did the same. Later we discovered that all three were fishermen who had been on the river the night we killed Janikowski. They had seen five men and a girl, a girl who wore her hair in plaits. (Danuta was the only one among our girls who did that.) They had also observed that one of the men had disappeared, while among the others there was one particularly tall one. (That was Olek.) So now the fishermen were able to identify at least two of us, and I was naturally arrested because of the bloodstained clothes.

Again we were asked what we knew about Janikowski and again we said that we knew nothing. They asked no more questions, but took us from the police station to the Mohács jail.

22

We spent five weeks in that jail, and they were the longest five weeks in my life. I was in a cell with Olek; the others were locked up separately. During the entire five weeks we got nothing to eat—that is, the prison authorities provided no food at all. Luckily we had some money of our own and the Hungarian girl who had helped us to forge our travel passes bought us enough to keep body and soul together. Even when our money was gone she continued to feed us at her own expense, or we would certainly have starved to death.

The cell had no furniture at all, not even a bench. We lay on the concrete floor with a single blanket. It was early spring and still rather cold.

On the second day we were again taken to be questioned. A

Ukrainian called Vasily Dumer acted as interpreter, translating our Polish into Hungarian.

The police officer asked me whether I would confess to the murder of Victor Janikowski. I said that I knew nothing whatsoever about it. We had agreed previously that should anything happen to us we would not speak or give away anything for at least two weeks, so that those who had managed to escape should not be traced and arrested and the headquarters in Budapest should not be raided. It was, we felt, most important that the work of the Hagana and of the Rescue Committee should not be interrupted. We assumed that they would move as quickly as they could, but we wanted to give them ample time to make whatever arrangements were necessary.

I was asked why my suit was stained with blood. I replied that I had lent it to my friend Starzow and couldn't say how he happened to get the blood on it. A few more questions and then I was taken into another cell and told to stand in a corner without moving. Soon a Hungarian gendarme entered and began to talk Magyar to me. I couldn't answer him, so he started to beat me with a whip, hitting my head and shoulders, shouting, "You've eaten Hungarian bread, but you haven't learned to speak Hungarian!"

(By then I could understand Magyar speech quite well, but still couldn't speak it very well.)

I didn't answer—he wouldn't have understood me in Polish, anyhow—and after a while he got tired of beating me. I was taken back to the cell I had shared with Olek and made to sit down in a corner; we were forbidden to talk. An hour later I was taken to interrogation again. After that they questioned us in the neighbouring room. Once again they asked about who had killed Janikowski. Once again I denied any knowledge of it. I felt more and more that if we could hold out the Hanoar Hazioni people who had been lucky enough to slip through the net in Mohács and Budapest would have a sporting chance of getting to Rumania.

When he saw that he wasn't getting anything out of me the police officer began to beat my hands with a bent stick. It hurt worse than anything I had felt before, and my hands started to swell almost immediately. He kept on repeating that he would beat me until I confessed. And I kept on saying that I had nothing to confess. He gave me twenty-five cuts over each hand. I collapsed. When I was able to move again they sent me back to the cell, and it was Olek's turn. After an hour he came back in the same condition. All six of us were interrogated in the same way. Danuta went through the same ordeal—and did not break down.

The third series of tortures began in the afternoon. A plain-clothes detective arrived who must have been a specialist. He told me that whatever they had done to us until now was just a mild foretaste of what was to come, and that he would show me all the tricks of persuasion he had learned or invented himself. He was certainly an expert. He fastened my hands with a strap, pushed a thick stick under my knees, and laid the stick across two chairs. I was hanging there like the carcass of a butchered animal, with my head near the floor and my legs on top. Soon he began to beat me with a rubber truncheon, concentrating on the soles of my feet. Again it was terribly painful and again I would not say anything. Olek went through the same ordeal, but he too refused to say anything. Neither did Danuta, and the others, of course, had nothing to say.

In the evening we were shackled together and driven back to our prison cells. Next day we could barely move, but they took us to the police station again, where they immediately started the interrogation. The same questions, the same answers, until it was like repeating parrot-fashion words that had lost their sense. Now the plain-clothes man, the "expert", made me take off my shoes and socks. Then he started to beat me on the bare soles. It seemed that I had shrunk into a body that was only a few square inches of skin where the pain was, everything else having disappeared. He went on beating me, my feet, my genitals. My feet became swollen; I could barely put on my shoes again. When it was over we had to walk back to the prison.

The torture lasted three days, almost unbroken. The journey from prison to police station, from the cell to the torture chamber, became harder and harder. Before it lasted only a few minutes; now it took more than half an hour. To us it felt like eternity, and every step caused almost unbearable pain.

On the fourth day the "expert" changed his method. He tied my hands at the back, stretched me on a bench, fastened my legs with straps to the top, bending them forward. Then he began to beat my naked feet again. When I started to scream (for the mere act of screaming helped) he gagged me with my

106

socks. This went on five or six times a day, with shorter or longer intervals. Every evening, half conscious, shackled, we had to drag ourselves back to the prison cell. The skin of my feet was split in several places and I was bleeding constantly; I could no longer put on my shoes and had to walk in the wet, blood-soaked socks.

We ate once a day, at noon, when we were given the food which Olek's Hungarian girl-friend provided. She was not allowed to visit us, but Tobka, another Polish girl, who was in the adjoining cellar, brought the food to us. She told us that Danuta was tortured in the same way as we were and that she had been able to hide in the stove in her cell the gun she had kept in her bra. Apart from Tobka, who told us how the others in our group had fared, we had one other contact with the world—the Ukrainian interpreter Vasily Dumer. Vasily was present at each interrogation, but he never laid a finger on us. On the contrary, he helped us as much as he could. He provided people in our group with some food (they were not as closely guarded as Olek, Danuta, and myself) and sometimes brought us a bit of his own bread-ration. Even more important, whenever he could he let me have a few puffs from his cigarette just before the torture began. He told us too that Danuta's gun hadn't been discovered. We asked him to collect it from her— we called it a mouth-organ, which was our slang for a gun— and Danuta handed it to him without a moment's hesitation. Thus she was no longer in any immediate danger, for if they had found the gun on her they would most likely have shot her at once. Dumer kept it for us.

After six days, during which he watched us being beaten for long hours, he could not stand it any longer. He asked to be relieved from his duty as an interpreter; he said his Polish wasn't good enough. His nerves were unable to endure witnessing our torment. Every beating lasted about half an hour, and this was repeated several times every day; on the average we received twenty-five or thirty blows on our soles. We were sorry that Vasily left, but we understood. We never saw him again.

At the end of a week we confessed that we had killed Victor Janikowski and explained our reasons for his execution. They wanted to know who gave us our orders and where those people could be found. We said that our orders had come from the headquarters of our group in Budapest, but we had no idea

107

of their address, as we had never been there, nor did we know the names of the people in charge.

On the eighth day a new detective arrived from Budapest. He sent for me, and when I arrived in the police captain's office he greeted me very politely, offered me a seat in a comfortable armchair, and even gave me a cigarette. Then he launched into a long speech about Hungarian-Polish friendship, how the two nations had always been brothers and had never fought against one another; he praised the patriotism of the Poles and talked about King Stephen Bathory, who was king both of Poland and Transylvania. After this, however, he became very business-like, again wanting to know who our leaders were, the address of the Polish Committee and its plans. I again told him that I knew nothing, but added that I was sorry he had come so late to Mohács, because if he had been here we probably would have been saved the sufferings and the "expertise" of his col-league. He said nothing, but sent me back to the cell, and Olek went through the same rigmarole. We knew it was the usual Gestapo method: when torture failed they tried phoney kind-ness. As it happened, it would have made no difference: with or without the beating we would have confessed to the killing of Victor Janikowski as soon as the confession did not jeopardize those of us who had managed to get away. We who were caught in the Nazi vice knew very well that there was little hope for us whatever we did or said.

Next day an SS man arrived. He was of medium height, with very clear blue eyes, quite a good-looking man. He spoke Polish with a Silesian accent.

"Are you Emil Tomaszkiewicz?" he asked.

"Yes."

"You are a Jew, from Tarnow, aren't you?"

"I am from Tarnow," I said, and added with pretended indignation, "but I am no Jew."

"I know you very well; you used to live in Ragojski Street."

"Then you must also know that I am not a Jew," I said. I was getting a little more self-confidence, for I realized that he was only bluffing: he had got all these details out of the first statement I had made. (We lived in Ursulanska Street; the *real* Tomaszkiewicz lived in Ragojski Street.)

He took me into another room. Before I entered he slapped me twice, hard.

"We'll see how long it is before you tell me the truth. You are a Jew."

I did not answer. Then he told me to say an *Ave Maria.* We had learned it in Budapest, just in case it was needed, so I recited it without a mistake.

"Now tell me the seven sacraments," he demanded.

I started off, but I got stuck after the fourth. He hit me again. I spat in his face and shouted, "If you don't believe that I am a Pole put me down for a Jew!"

"I'll show you, you filthy pig, what you are! I'll beat you to a pulp!"

He forced me down across a chair, straddled my back, and began to beat me with a rubber truncheon, screaming that he would go on beating until I confessed. When I kept silent he pulled down my trousers and beat me around my genitals with a wet cloth. I was still silent, for if I had told him anything more than we had already confessed it would still have involved too many people. After an hour I was taken back to the cell; I had to be dragged along, for I could no longer walk. Then it was Olek's turn. The SS man obviously enjoyed his work, for he repeated the dose twice more, though he got less and less pleasure out of it because both Olek and I lost consciousness fairly quickly in the proceedings.

In the evening we were taken back to prison. We were unable to walk or sit. Our whole bodies were a mass of bruises and there were many wounds that were bleeding.

In the next cell there were some German prisoners, SS men who had been locked up for minor disciplinary breaches, just being held there until they were sent on to Budapest. They could move freely in the corridors, and when they saw us through the spy-hole of our cell they made one of the turnkeys open the door and gave us cigarettes. One of them said, "We've been in the Warsaw ghetto, but even there they didn't beat people like you've been beaten." The Hungarian warders also took pity on us and brought food and some ointment for our wounds, to stop the bleeding and ease the pain.

But the torture still went on. Now the two of us, Olek and I, were tied together on a bench. Two men came and started to beat the soles of our feet with rubber truncheons; then they stabbed our private parts with sharp pencils, while slapping our faces and hammering on our skulls. They did this until we fainted, then poured water over us, and the SS man asked,

"Well, have you got anything to say?"

We kept silent. So he said, "Why should I and my men tire ourselves beating you? You beat each other!"

But of course we wouldn't: even if we had wanted to we hadn't any strength left.

"I'll show you, pigs!" he said, and took Olek, removed his trousers, and beat him again with a wet towel, with whips, sticks, anything he could find that was sharp and hard. As he stood over him Olek suddenly lifted his head and butted him in the stomach with all his might, so that he fell over. This made him go berserk. He smashed Olek's teeth, he pummelled his chest so hard that he began to spit blood and fainted. Then he picked up a piece of wood and beat both of us. We were really nothing more than two swollen, shapeless masses of sores and wounds.

At this point they brought a doctor to revive us. He came and found that Olek had two broken fingers on his left hand and that my right leg was badly injured. He looked at us, but said nothing. Our feet were monstrously swollen, for the SS man kept us through long nights with our legs in ice-cold water and our ankles were slashed. Later we found out that the doctor had told the SS man that if he continued beating us we would die within a day; he left the decision to him, naturally, but hinted that he would make a report that might be unpleasant. So they stopped beating us.

In the meantime they had once taken us to the Danube to reconstruct the killing of Janikowski. That gave us a chance to talk to the Hungarian girl who was Olek's sweetheart. From her we learned that the other members of our group had been released and had left for Budapest. Whether they did this because they were satisfied with our partial confession, making us entirely responsible for the execution of Janikowski, or whether they hoped that the others would lead them to the Hagana headquarters, I couldn't say. In any case, this strengthened us in our resolve that we wouldn't tell them anything more, for the people in Budapest needed a margin of safety to escape and to wipe out all traces that could lead to their arrest.

After a couple of days the SS man with the blue eyes came into the cell. He no longer tried to talk Polish, but addressed me in German.

"Have you had breakfast today?" he asked.

"No. Not yet."

"I am sorry," he said. "That's gross negligence. You'll get it right away!"

And he forced me to drink a glass of water with a lot of salt in it. He told the policeman who was guarding us, "Be careful! He mustn't have anything to drink, not a drop of water! And nothing to eat!"

He did the same with Olek. At lunchtime he came back and said, "Have you had your lunch yet?"

I said I hadn't.

"Well, now you should have two courses"—he grinned—"and I hope you'll like them both!"

He had two glasses of water with about one third salt in them. I refused to drink. He tied me to a bench, forced my head back, and poured the contents of the two glasses down my throat. The same thing happened to Olek. By the afternoon we were lying on the floor, unable to speak or move, tormented by such an unbearable thirst that I thought there was a fire burning in my guts.

That fire was to burn for a long time. The SS man with the blue eyes had said, "This is what you're going to get for fourteen days until all your guts are seared to cinders. Maybe then you'll start talking."

I croaked, "I won't . . ."

That was the last time I spoke for the next three days. My tongue was cleaving to the roof of my mouth, my throat, my lips, were as dry as if they were caked with salt. In the evening he came again and said, "Why should I really ask you whether you've had dinner, when you're bound to tell me you didn't even get breakfast? One glass of salt and water for the gentlemen!"

Again he forced it down my gullet, and Olek's. He accompanied us to the toilet to make sure that nobody gave us anything to eat or drink.

During the night it was getting much worse. The gendarmes who guarded us now had orders not to let us go to the W.C., and inside the stabbing, burning pain grew and grew. This torture went on for three days. Again and again the SS man told us that he would let us go as soon as we told him the address of our organization in Budapest and the names of its members. But we were still silent. On the third day he promised us to go on with the "water-cure" until we had no intestines left. We still did not speak.

111

On the fourth morning he arrived early in the torture-cellar. We were no longer being transferred every evening from the police station to the prison, as we couldn't move.

"Well, the cure didn't work." He smiled. "So let's try a little shock treatment. I'll put on a nice concert for you, to teach you how many different ways there are to beat people."

He dragged me into the torture room, and they beat me for two hours without pause, taking turns. Olek was brought in a few minutes later, and they went to work on him at the same time. When we became unconscious they stopped because we couldn't feel anything any more. They threw us in a cell, and that's where I came to a few hours later.

The SS man came in and said, "Well, now you'll get a little peace. We're going to put you on trial, just to make it legal before we hang you . . . what's left of you."

This was the twenty-fourth day since our arrest, and the twenty-second of our almost constant torment. After the SS man had left one of our guards brought us a jug of water and a piece of bread. We forced ourselves to eat and drink very slowly, taking five minutes or so between each bite and sip. We were still dazed and sore, but somehow we recovered our senses, at least sufficiently to talk. I crawled over to Olek, and we agreed that if we were hanged we would sing the anthem *Jessne Polska nie Sioneta* to show that we were true patriots. But even as we discussed this and made feeble little jokes about not being able to sing in tune, I somehow could not believe that they would hang us. It was a stupid, irrational feeling and it turned out to be completely right.

23

Early next morning the gendarmes came and told us to get dressed. We were taken into a large room where a lady sat behind a typewriter, while behind a long table we saw Captain Albert, two civilians, and our "friendly" SS man. They had some papers in front of them.

The Captain said, "Well, you can tell us your last wish."

I said I wanted to write a letter to my mother. They gave me paper and pencil and I wrote a short letter, saying that I was being hanged for killing a Jew who had betrayed his own kind and because I was fighting for the freedom of Poland. They asked whether we wanted anything else. I asked for a priest, but they said that was impossible. Then the SS man said there was one last chance: if we gave the names, they would pardon us. I shook my head and started to sing the anthem. I was still singing when they put a rope around my neck. "This is your very last chance!" the SS man said again. I went on singing. He tightened the rope and started to pull. I immediately lost consciousness. They obviously did not pull the rope quite tight, nor did they raise me very high, for I came to and heard the SS man scream, "These Polish bastards, these bandits, you can beat them to death and still they won't talk!"

He gave me a few more blows with his whip, and then started on Olek. Then the gendarmes carried me and the others back to the cellar.

The whole business about the death sentence and the pretended hanging was just a trick to frighten us into talking. It failed just as the beating and the salt-and-water torture had failed. But now the time limit which we had set for ourselves had passed (we weren't quite certain whether it was twenty-one or twenty-three days, for time had become blurred by pain and unconsciousness), and we decided with Olek that there was no harm in telling a little of what we knew. We asked for the Hungarian plain-clothes man who had been kind to us, for we did not want to give the SS torturer the satisfaction of being given the information. We told him the address of the committee in Budapest and the plans to leave the country, though no details about the escape route. He was very polite and friendly. Later they checked at the address and found that the Hagana and the Waad Hahacala people had actually stayed there, but had gone long ago. The Hungarian police would have liked to know where they had moved to: *we* knew that the whole organization had been transferred to Rumania. We had given them ample time to wind up everything in Hungary, and we felt that it had been worth while to endure all we had suffered for the sake of the others.

24

A few days later we were transferred from Mohács to the prison in Pécs. Here the whole atmosphere was different. Olek and I were in one block, though not on the same floor; Danuta was in a cell on the top floor, quite separate from us because she was so young, not yet seventeen. Not that she had a particularly easy time: she had to share her cell with prostitutes, gipsy girls, and all kinds of strange creatures.

The day after we arrived in Pécs they took us to the prison governor's office and read out the indictment. Apparently we had been sentenced to death, but the carrying out of the sentence was postponed until another hearing had been held. This was rather putting the cart before the horse, but we certainly did not mind. At least we were alive and were no longer beaten.

Not that life was all that pleasant in jail. In my cell there was a bed, a table, a chair, and a bucket. During the whole day I was forbidden to lie down on the bed or even sit on it. I was allowed only to sit on the chair with my hands in my lap or to walk up and down. It wasn't much of a walk—three and a half steps one way and the same back. The tiny, barred window, half covered with a sheet of tin, showed only a palm-size patch of sky.

The prison routine was fairly monotonous. They woke us at five-thirty; we emptied our buckets and then went to the washroom. We were given only ten minutes to clean up, then back to the cell. Breakfast, with fifteen minutes' exercise before lunch. The prison was built on the hillside, so we had to climb to the fourth floor to reach the courtyard in which we could move in a circle, our hands behind our backs, keeping a strictly prescribed distance from each other, two lines, clockwise and anti-clockwise. After lunch we had to sit again on our hard chairs until dinner; we could lie down only after lights out. Sometimes I tossed and turned half the night, for I was young and needed much more physical exercise to be properly tired. In order to make the sameness of our days endurable, I started to learn Hungarian from a Polish–Hungarian dictionary which I got from a prison visitor, a woman who belonged to some missionary society.

114

The food wasn't exactly lavish. For breakfast we got a so-called soup—water with a little flour and a good deal of hot red pepper. When we first got it I found it so spicy that I couldn't force it down, so I ate only the few ounces of bread that went with it and poured away the rest. But later I became used to it—even today I love *paprika*. At first I thought they gave it to us in order to continue the torture which the SS man had invented, but I found out that all prisoners got the same. For lunch we had bean soup—that is, water with about three broad beans—and dinner was the same soup with one potato. They also gave us coffee, or, rather, dirty water miscalled coffee. Only on Sundays did we get some macaroni and broad-bean soup with a few bits of meat. On Sundays, too, we were taken to church to attend Mass. No-one seemed to think that we were Jews. Our false identity papers were accepted here, and our confession about our connection with the Hagana had apparently not been passed on or communicated to the prison authorities.

In the meantime Tusia Herzberg, a member of our original group who had stayed in Budapest, was doing everything to get us out. Hungary was now totally in the German grip and things were very difficult. Tusia, who was now known as Jadwiga, had perfect forged papers as a nurse working for the Swiss Red Cross, and she was able to visit us several times. She even managed to get us a lawyer, a Dr Király, who was willing to defend us if and when we had a court trial.

It was Jadwiga who thought up another daring attempt to free us. Some time in August three of our friends who had also stayed in Hungary, Piotr Rostowiecki, Tadek Lublinski and Dudek Maslowski, turned up in Pécs in the car of the Turkish Ambassador. (Dudek, with forged Aryan papers, was working as a driver at the Turkish Embassy.) They were dressed in SS uniforms and carried cleverly forged orders to deliver Olek and myself into their hands. Unfortunately they did not have a counter-signature from the Gestapo and the Governor of the prison refused their demand. (It was much later that we found out about it. If Piotr and Tadek had been caught they would have been shot by the Germans on the spot.) They did not have much time to argue—there was always the risk that the Governor might telephone Budapest—so, pretending to be angry over such "insubordination", they drove away.

Meanwhile I was regularly getting into trouble. The Russians were approaching the Danube, having destroyed the Hungarian armies, and the Germans were beginning their long rearguard action in Hungary. At the same time both the Western Allies and the Russians were bombing important railway and industrial targets, of which Pécs was one. During the air raids Olek and I were taken downstairs into the prison cellar, which served as a shelter, and here we met other prisoners. Some of them were allowed to smoke, and I was in agony, watching them puffing away, for I had become an addict long before we came to Hungary. I could not resist the temptation and bartered my shirt for two cigarettes. One I smoked on the spot; I became quite dizzy, but I enjoyed it tremendously. The other I took into my cell and smoked next day. But a guard caught me and took me immediately to the Governor's office. He promptly gave me ten days' solitary.

I had grown a little soft and my wounds had healed, so it was harder than ever before to endure it. My hands were tied to my legs and I had to sit on the bare stone floor in a small cell which had no light. I was fed only every second day—some bread and water. They took me, however, for the regular exercise every day, and after the first it was excruciating to have to climb the stairs to the fourth floor. During the seven months I spent in Pécs, from April to November 1944, I had three spells in solitary, twice because of smoking and once because I climbed up to my window to get my bearings as to the position of my cell in the prison complex.

We waited for our trial, but it was postponed again and again. One day in October a Gestapo official arrived and demanded, "Where are the Poles?"

We were rounded up and taken to an office where a Hungarian doctor made us take off our trousers and kept looking at us. Then he said, "You can go."

They escorted us back to the prison, where soon the rumours began to fly that the "Poles" were really Jews. But no-one was quite sure. After the war we met the Hungarian doctor, Dr Molnár, who told us: "The Gestapo wanted to know whether you were circumcised or not. So I told them that you were, but it was through some operation—I couldn't quite establish the cause, it might have been an accident—and said that there were plenty of Gentiles in Eastern Europe who had their boys circumcised for hygienic reasons."

25

Late in November the air raids on Pécs became intensified. Most of the attacks were now by Russian planes. Inside the prison we heard that the Russians had crossed the Danube and were sweeping through Western Hungary and that Yugoslav partisan forces had also crossed the Drava, the great Danube tributary, and were approaching Pécs.

On November 21st all prisoners who had less than a year left of their sentences were released. Four days later we began to hear gunfire, still some distance away, but coming closer. That night shells started to land close to the prison. The guards, who had been grim and unfriendly in the past, now began to talk to us, to ingratiate themselves. We got extra rations. On November 26th one of the prisoners who had been released came back to the jail. He said he did not know where to go because his native village, some ten miles from Pécs, was already occupied by the Russians. This caused considerable panic among the warders and the gendarmes. Some of them disappeared.

Then, on November 28th, several Gestapo men came to the prison and declared that next day all political prisoners would be shot. All of us were then herded into one large cell, about forty people, among them seven or eight Yugoslav partisans. There was not much reaction to this announcement: somehow, having survived so much, we couldn't believe that on the threshold of freedom we would be destroyed. This belief had no foundation in reality; all we could do was to wait. Some prayed; I managed to get half a dozen cigarettes from one of the Yugoslavs and portioned them out so they lasted me the whole night, for there was no question of sleep. Just before midnight we heard the German tanks and lorries rumble past, and we thought they were leaving. No-one came near us. Then, a few hours later, the same vehicles seemed to come back again. We waited, holding our breath. But they passed the prison without stopping.

The winter dawn was very slow and reluctant. We dozed off a little. It was about seven-thirty in the morning when a com-

117

plete, deathly silence descended upon the town. It was broken now and then by scattered machine-gun fire. After a while we heard the rumble of tanks, at first in the distance, then closer and closer, until they seemed directly outside. Two men lifted me up so that I could look out of the window.

I saw some tanks completely covered in mud so that their markings were obliterated. I couldn't tell whether they were German or Russian. After another few minutes we heard heavy footsteps. Now I saw the first Russian soldiers, with automatic pistols in their hands, walking gingerly along the walls of the houses opposite.

I cleared my throat and wanted to shout. But at first no sound came, I was so excited and weak. I tried very hard; at first it was a croak, and then, just as the Russians had almost disappeared round the corner, I managed to call out with all my strength.

"Here!" I shouted. "Political prisoners! Come and help us!"

It looked as if they hadn't heard me, so I repeated the same words. Two of them turned and looked up. I waved and shouted again.

They crossed the streets at a run and, firing a burst, shot off the lock. A gendarme who was standing in the passage was killed on the spot; a little later we saw his body. They came pounding down the corridor and a few minutes later we were free. There was much shouting and crying, some embraced the Russians, one or two performed a strange little dance of exhilaration.

After giving us some bread and a bottle of Hungarian apricot brandy they must have picked up somewhere, the Russians left. They were front-line troops and had to press on. By the time they arrived there were no Germans left in Pécs. The Gestapo men made themselves scarce only a short time before the entry of the Russian troops. In the main courtyard there were chalk-marks on the brick wall where they had intended to line us up for execution. The former prisoners disarmed the guards, the Governor, and his deputies and escorted them to the Russian town command post.

We were free.

26

Olek and I had had plenty of time to discuss what we would
do if we survived the Nazi terror, if we lived long enough in
spite of the beatings and the salt-water torture, to start settling
accounts. We had both seen children, women, and old men
mowed down by machine-guns; we saw the swollen bellies of
the hungry children in the ghettoes, looking, grotesquely, as if
they were nine months pregnant. Quite independently of each
other, we had both decided that if we were given the chance
we would not waste any time—no, not a second.

The first thing we did when we were let out of that cell was
to get ourselves guns; we picked up some which had been taken
from the disarmed guards, carefully choosing the best weapons
for which there was most ammunition available. We could
barely walk. My weight had dropped to less than eighty pounds
—nearer seventy. Olek was not much fatter: he was so very
tall that he looked even more of a skeleton. The next thing was
to find out the private address of the Hungarian colonel who
was responsible for the deportation and massacre of the Jews
in Pécs. We had heard enough hair-raising stories about him in
prison; we knew his name and we had a full score against him.

The Russians had arrived about seven-thirty. By half-past
eight we were in the apartment of the Colonel. His wife was at
home, but he had obviously gone. We searched the whole
place, every corner and closet. In the pantry whole sides of
bacon, lengths of salami, smoked sausages, and hams were
hanging. It was only then we realized that we hadn't eaten anything, for we didn't even pause to munch the bread the Russians
had given us. But we did not touch any of the food, not in that
pantry. However, when we were leaving Olek and I noticed a
pair of fur gloves on the hall table. It was freezing outside and
a snowstorm was just beginning; without much thought, we
took them.

But when we got back to the prison, we decided that it was
wrong to take anything—no matter how badly we had been
treated. And so, after a little supper, we trudged back.

It was almost midnight when we rang the bell at the Colonel's apartment. His wife came to the door, white-faced with fright, shivering in a robe. Olek just handed her the gloves.

"I'm sorry. We took these by mistake."

"But please . . . have them if you want them. Anything you like."

"No, thank you," I said.

We went away. We were shivering ourselves now as we trudged back to the prison, and we felt rather foolish. But we also felt better.

27

Next morning Olek, Danuta, and I went to Colonel Gorada, who was the Russian commandant of Pécs. We took two of the Hungarian prison guards with us who had been particularly nasty to us and whom we had kept locked up in one of our former cells overnight.

As I spoke the best Russian, I was the spokesman. The Colonel, a bearded giant of a man, looked at us and said, "And who the hell are you?"

"A Pole and a former political prisoner," I said. "These two have been with me in jail, and these are our former guards who are war criminals."

"Am I supposed to believe that?"

I told him the rest of our story, and he listened pleasantly enough. At the end he said, "That's a very fine tale, but how do I know it's true? What about the guns you carry? Where did you get them?"

We explained and he ordered us to hand them over, which we did, rather reluctantly. For the guns were the tangible proof that we were free, that no-one could now tell us what to do or say.

However, we had no choice. We were taken back to the prison and kept there for three days, though we were not locked in cells and had enough to eat—even cigarettes.

On the fourth day the Colonel sent for us.

"I've checked your story," he said. "Not all of it, there isn't time. You seem to have told the truth. Would you like to work for us?"

"What work?" I asked, a bit suspiciously. "We want to fight the Germans."

"You can do that by helping us to round up the war criminals. Officially you'll be interpreters. I understand, Tomaszkiewicz, you speak Hungarian besides Polish and German, don't you? Good. We'll give you proper rank, uniforms, and pay, and you'll report to me personally."

That was okay with us. Within a few days we were in Russian uniforms. I was actually given the temporary, acting, unofficial rank of a lieutenant, and so was Olek, and we started our work. In those days if we arrested any Germans we handed them over to the Russian Intelligence Service. As the Soviet armies surged westwards we followed them through Hungary and Austria, then back into Rumania. Our work began early in December 1944 and ended in October 1945.

Until the official end of the war, which was May 8th, 1945, under the general orders of the Russians, any Germans, Austrians, or Hungarians accused or suspected of Nazi affiliations or war crimes were sent to the Soviet Union to be tried. The civilian population was treated somewhat harshly: all men between sixteen and forty-five, all women between eighteen and forty, were sent east for forced labour. Of course, when I say all I mean those who were caught in the net of the Russian armies, for many went into hiding or escaped west, preferring to become prisoners of the Western Allies. But at a rough guess well over a million Hungarians, Austrians, and Germans were crowded into freight-trains and shipped east. Some of them never returned; many came back only after several years.

People were divided up according to their national origins, which made our task easier. In Hungary I worked in Kaposvár and a number of other Transdanubian towns and villages before I moved to Austria with my detachment. We combed the German-speaking, so-called Swabian villages which had been originally settled by order of the Empress Maria Theresa after the end of the Turkish wars in the late eighteenth century. We talked to people, drew them out, checked and counter-checked their statements. It wasn't really difficult. Many among them pointed out this or that man and said, "He was with the Arrow Cross, the Hungarian Nazis . . . that one was in command of a Jewish labour battalion . . . this one was a guard in the ghetto." They denounced one another with the greatest readiness, even enthusiasm. Sometimes, though rarely, it turned out that they did this in order to cover up for their own misdeeds or for personal revenge. Though we were under pressure to make the arrests quickly and not let anybody escape who deserved to be rounded up, we did our best to get at least two or three independent witnesses, and, of course, sometimes the surviving victims of these ex-Nazis and SS men could be found to testify against them. There were photographs, too, which they had had taken proudly, in their Arrow Cross or SS uniforms.

It was a job which I enjoyed with all my heart. I was eager to do it well, and I knew that it would last a long time, though I wasn't quite sure how long I could carry on myself, for already I was beginning to feel a little restless. And then, in Nagykanizsa, a Hungarian Jew gave us some details about a German who had worked with the SS and the Hungarian Nazis and who had personally shot over a hundred Hungarian Jewish children.

It took us some time to track him down, for he changed his hide-out every day, never sleeping in the same place two nights running. He had grown a beard and was sometimes dressed in a monk's habit, sometimes in the uniform of a Hungarian fireman. He knew that we were looking for him, and I suppose he hoped that he would establish contact with the organization which the Nazis had set up long before the end of the war and which helped so many of them to escape to South America and other places.

In the end we caught him in a brewery where he was working as a night watchman. He did not put up much of a fight, though he kept on saying that we were mistaken, that he was somebody else. He had, of course, forged papers, but we shaved him and the Jew (who had actually watched his two small sons being killed by this man) identified him without a moment's hesitation.

We turned him over to the Russians, who put him under arrest.

Two days later as I was walking down the main street of Nagykanizsa I met him walking along as bold as brass. He was still wearing the same clothes in which we had arrested him. I followed him round the corner, then took out my gun and shot him dead.

28

The Russian military police arrested me and took me to the local *Kommandatur*. I was kept waiting for a few hours, then Colonel Gorada walked in and started to shout at me, "Have you gone mad, Tomaszkiewicz? Killing a man in the middle of a busy street!"

"He was a murderer who had escaped. I killed him because he deserved it."

"What were you thinking of? Are you setting up your own personal court of justice and carrying out your own executions?"

"But, Colonel..."

"You are working for us, not for yourself. As long as you are in the Russian Army you'll obey our rules and stick to our regulations. You are under arrest."

I was very angry, but of course I couldn't do anything. I was taken to a guardroom and had to give up my arms. I was kept there for three days, but well provided with food, drink, and cigarettes. Then, on the evening of the third day, the Colonel's second-in-command came to see me. I had not had many dealings with him in the past, for the Colonel had told me always to report to him directly. He was an older man, very soft-spoken and sad-looking.

"Well now, Emil," he said, "tell me all about this German."

So I told him all I had discovered, how I had tracked him down and arrested him, and how surprised and upset I was when I saw him at large.

"Why do you think he had been released?" the Captain asked.

"I don't know. He probably told a lot of lies."

"No. We let him go on purpose."

"Then you did wrong. You should have hanged him right away."

"We let him go because we thought he'd lead us to bigger game, more important people. Have you heard of a man called Eichmann?"

"No."

"Eichmann was the man who organized the rounding up of the Jews in Hungary, Poland, Czechoslovakia, who arranged the transport to the death-camps. We thought that your German worked for him and knew where he was. And he might very well have known where Eichmann is hiding. There are other big Nazis we think are still alive—even Bormann, the Fuehrer's deputy, though some say he was killed in the final days of the battle for Berlin. So, you see, it was a stupid thing for you to kill your SS man."

"But why didn't the Colonel tell me?"

"Maybe he would have if you'd been here. But you were away, remember? And how could the Colonel have known that you would shoot him?"

He looked at me, then reached under his cape and brought out my gun.

"Here, you can have it back."

"You mean, I am no longer under arrest?"

"No. I think you did what you thought was right. And one Nazi less won't make that much difference."

He smiled and held out his hand. It was only later that I found out he was a Jew whose whole family had been killed by the Germans in Kiev.

29

We moved steadily westwards. After the end of the European war the Russians changed their treatment of the Germans and Austrians. They were not to be treated so severely any more; I suppose, though this is something of hindsight, that Moscow wanted to gain some support in the Eastern Zone that was to be established in Potsdam. But our work continued: we were still ferreting out SS men and Gestapo officials. But if someone was to be arrested we had to call in the Russian field police and they made the actual arrest. Many were released fairly soon; others were tried by regular, legal courts which the Russians set up. They were no longer subjected to prolonged beatings, nor were they being led through the streets in large groups before deportation. The trains were still rolling eastwards, but they were loaded at night; the Russians obviously wanted to avoid antagonizing the population too much, for they needed them to work, to help restore communications, prevent a terrible famine that first post-war winter. They treated the conquered more gently, more humanely, at least so it seemed to us.

Russian Intelligence continued to look for contacts, to gather witnesses against the many thousands of war criminals still at large. I was sent several times to Yugoslavia to discuss these things with some investigators there, to take depositions and collect material. Some people came from Bulgaria to help. There was no country in Central and Eastern Europe which did not have a terrible account to settle.

Early in October the Colonel sent for me.

"Tomaszkiewicz," he said, "we are handing over our work to the security police. I want you to come back with us to Russia, and then we will be moving to Japan."

"Japan?" I couldn't help being surprised. "What would I be doing in Japan?"

"The same kind of intelligence work. Some of the Nazis may have fled there. It will be a worth-while and interesting job. I'll see to it that you get your rank confirmed, your status regularized."

The last thing I wanted was to become a Russian officer or to go to Japan. But I knew I couldn't tell him that.

"You would like that, wouldn't you?" he asked.

"Yes, Colonel," I lied. "But could I have some leave now? It isn't so many months ago that I came out of jail and I haven't had a chance to find out what has happened to my mother, to my family."

He looked at me, narrowing his eyes.

"I could have some inquiries made."

"But that might take a long time. If I could have two weeks . . ."

"Well . . ." He hesitated. "I cannot authorize leave for you to Poland. But you can have two weeks in Rumania, and as long as you report to our office in Moscow by November 10th you can do what you like in the meantime. It won't be easy to travel from Rumania to Poland, but you're a resourceful fellow and you might just do it. Remember—November 10th! Don't be late!"

"No, of course not," I promised.

I collected some pay and travel papers. It took me about four days to get to Bucharest. I did not know anybody, but I found the ruined synagogue and there met some Jews. At first, seeing my Russian uniform, they were very reserved. But I reassured them and they passed me on to the local Hagana organization, where I met some of the Hanoar Hazioni group, several of whom had been with me on that terrible journey from Poland into Hungary.

They were happy to see me, and not long afterwards Olek and Danuta also arrived from Hungary. They told me that there was a ship sailing in ten days' time from Constanza, the first ship carrying legal immigrants to Palestine. It was called the *Transylvania* and carried a thousand passengers.

Of course, these were proper immigrants with the right kind of documents, while I had nothing of the sort. But I had my army pay which I had saved up and I had collected a suitcase full of scarce items, such as razor-blades, tea, coffee, and even aspirins. (All these were still in very short supply in Rumania.) The difficulty was to find out whom to bribe and with how much, so that he would stay bribed.

I found out that the embarkation was in the charge of a Rumanian (not a Jew) who had expensive tastes. These included, of all things, silk underwear, though he was the first man I'd heard of wanting that luxury. Through a member in our group I found a black marketeer who had silk underwear to sell, not for money, which was worth very little, but for goods. My suitcase was half emptied before I acquired the necessary "twin sets"—silk undershirts and drawers. This was a useful division, for I told the man that I would give him one or the other, and the rest only when the ship had sailed. (He was coming with us as a purser.) He agreed. The travel documents were much easier. I cast off my Russian uniform and with the help of the Hagana reduced myself from the rank of major to that of a humble civilian called Roman Branicki. I hoped my Russian colonel would not be too disappointed if I did not report for duty and did not go to Japan.

30

It was October 27th, 1945, a little after my twenty-first birthday, when I landed in what was still called Palestine. It was the Sabbath, and I felt that the rest of my life would be one long holiday now. I was completely alone in the world: not even the most distant kinsman of mine had survived the holocaust, though I had some friends. They were kind and considerate, but still they weren't family.

I was a little drunk with the feeling that I was alive and that the country of which we had spoken and dreamt so much in Tarnow, on our long journey across Poland and Hungary, in the prisons of Mohács and Pécs, was now mine, under my feet and all around me. I almost felt that I had to touch myself and the sand, the rocks, the walls of the houses, to make certain that everything was real.

The group to which I belonged decided to join the same kibbutz, called Tel Icchak, about twenty-five miles from Tel Aviv. I had some skills which they could use: I could drive, repair, and even make things; my years in the technical school and the months I worked with my father in Stanislawow and Kolomyja came in useful now. We did not have exclusive, specialist tasks: we turned our hands to whatever was needed. And we learned Hebrew, studying hard.

The great war was over now—even Japan had surrendered. I sometimes wondered whether my Russian colonel and his detachment had ever got to Tokyo or the Far East. I began to read the papers and soon realized that the fight was not yet over, that my war might be just beginning again. I read that Truman and Attlee were about to issue some agreed statement on the Arab-Jewish problem; that Ibn Saud, the King of Saudi Arabia, threatened to cancel the American oil concessions if the American President continued his "anti-Arab" stand. I didn't quite know what oil had to do with the Jews coming to Palestine, but before long I learned. It was said that twenty-five thousand Jews would be allowed to enter, but that did not seem so very many to me. Another newspaper stated that ninety-five thousand wanted to come from Europe alone. There was even a report about our own landing at Haifa: we were supposed to be the "last large group" allowed to come in. There were two American senators, Wagner and Taft, who called for unlimited admission of Jews. I thought it a pity that they were not in the place of Attlee and Truman, but then, perhaps, they would have talked differently. And one paper, which I could not quite believe, said that anti-Semitism was growing in Poland and even the few thousand Jews who had survived might be forced to emigrate. I couldn't believe it for two reasons. Hadn't the Poles and the Jews suffered together under the Nazis? Would any Jews have to be "forced" to leave? If I could judge by myself they would be only too eager to go.

A few days after we settled down in the kibbutz my friend Dudek came to me and said, "You are going to join the Hagana, aren't you?"

"If they want me."

"They want everybody who can fire a gun or dig a ditch. We may have to start fighting—tomorrow or next year, nobody knows—but we must be prepared."

"All I need is to be told."

"Don't go to sleep tomorrow evening. We may be needed for a special mission. Then you can prove that you are fit to be in the Hagana."

I kept awake and about eleven o'clock Dudek came for me. Outside the kibbutz gates a lorry was waiting and we climbed on board. There were already half a dozen people, all men, on it. They gave us masks, cut out of cardboard with bits of string attached to them, but we were not armed.

I asked Dudek where we were going.

"To help some people to join us."

"What people?"

"Our people. They have no permits, no papers, so they need a little help."

We drove for about forty minutes, then stopped in an orange-grove. We were told to put on our masks. Dudek explained that this was simply to avoid being identified later should any of the illegal immigrants be caught and frightened into a confession. I didn't need to be told more; I knew that it was a sensible precaution.

Then I found myself lying on top of a steep cliff along the coast, watching blinking signals in the inky darkness far out to sea. Invisible figures on the shore answered and Dudek's voice said, "Now!"

Several rowing-boats put out from the lee shore with muffled oars. With my invisible companions I waited half an hour until the boats approached the shore again, this time stopping within wading distance. Joining the others, I waded out through the lukewarm water, with waves slapping around my chest. I carried back a small, whimpering girl who clung to me in terror. Although I tried every language I knew, I couldn't soothe her

128

fears, but when I reached the wet sand a woman came forward to take over her care.

While I was wading ashore there was some altercation a couple of yards from me. A burly man, carrying another thin figure pick-a-back, suddenly stopped and asked gruffly, "What's that squirming in your rucksack?"

A reedy voice replied in Yiddish, "It's Schnucki!"

"And who may Schnucki be?" demanded the other man.

"It's my dog, my only companion. Four years I carried him with me. He is the only thing I have."

"A dog!" snorted my fellow-member of the "reception committee". "Have you gone crazy? You think I am going to risk prison or internment camp for a dog? Here . . ." He reached back, yanked the rucksack from the other man's shoulders, and threw it into the sea. I heard the splash and saw the rucksack, writhing and struggling with a muffled whine as the waves buffeted it in the faint starlight.

On the shore the thin little man set up a piteous wailing. He said he would rather die, he would rush back into the sea this very moment if Schnucki were to be killed. He explained volubly how wonderful Schnucki was, how clever, how good, how modest. The burly man, still wearing his mask, who had carried him to safety listened for a few moments, then dashed back into the water and retrieved Schnucki. He shook the dog out of the rucksack—it was a small dachshund, rather the worse for wear—and muttered, shaking his head, "These people! These incredible people!"

The unloading took two hours, and then the ship turned and disappeared silently out to sea. The boats, too, had vanished and the immigrants were herded up a steep path towards a winding road. After more than an hour's walk we came to a large barn-like building where a meal was ready and dry clothes available.

They were told where they should go. Though the lights were dim and we still wore our masks, the practical sense and the nonchalance of all the people who had organized the illegal landing and of the new arrivals themselves made the situation seem perfectly commonplace. I even felt as if I had been doing this many times, rather than being a relative newcomer myself.

People living in the houses on the shore, Dudek told me, were often awakened in the middle of the night and asked to put up four or five arrivals. No questions were ever asked: the immigrants were supplied with food and clothing and at dawn their dispersal began. Some found refuge in the agricultural settlements, others mingled unobtrusively in the big towns, while still others were smuggled into villages. There was no reliable check on the population in Palestine. Now and then the official registers and police offices were destroyed by bombs. Care was always taken to time the bombs so as not to hurt anybody.

Every detail of the arrival of these ships was carefully planned, nothing left to chance. True, the British Navy was supposed to keep a sharp watch off the coast, but the coastline was too long for really effective patrolling and the British authorities were unwilling to apply extreme measures such as sinking a ship or driving it ashore.

By the time I arrived myself there were some 18,000 officially registered illegal immigrants. I was told that the real number was about five times greater.

And all through the winter months of 1945-6 I helped to add to the total.

31

Though no-one could threaten us with injury or death, I soon became aware that our fight was far from ended. In a way we led a double life, sometimes sharply separated, sometimes closely linked. We worked at our varied jobs in the kibbutzim while we were training for the inevitable clash that was coming. Some of my original group had joined the Irgun Zwai Leumi and one became a member of the Stern Group. But I did not feel like becoming associated with either of them. I was content to join the Hagana to which Dudek and some others, less inclined to extremism, belonged.

In those first months I travelled all over Palestine to become acquainted with my new country which I knew was to be my final home.

I travelled to Haifa and Jerusalem, to Tiberias and to Tel Aviv, but above all I tried to visit as many of the kibbutzim as I could. I went to Ein Geb, on the far side of Lake Galilee or Kinneret, a fishing and agricultural settlement which was founded in 1936—quite old for a Palestinian community. It lay between the mountains and the lake, hemmed in by both: marauding Arabs often came across the hills of Transjordan and the settlement was in a state of constant alert. They made me welcome in the little brick pavilion which was open to the breeze and where they entertained visitors. Their buildings were scattered over the slope of the gently rising hill. They had built a stone jetty for the fishing-fleet and another open shed housed the nets; they repaired and made their own and were engaged at the time of my visit in building a large motor-boat to make fishing more economical. Proudly, they showed me their ice-plant, the cisterns, the family houses, the dining-hall, and the watch-tower. Besides fishing and growing fruit-trees and wheat—huge yellow stacks of straw stacked in the only level field proved that they had had a good harvest—Ein Geb also turned out gravel and metal-work. About three hundred people lived and worked there, and they seemed to be happier than any I had met in Europe. They took me up to the library, almost on top of the hill. It was a clean, neat building with large glass walls and a brick roof. Its walls were covered with book jackets, for at that time all over Palestine the settlements held exhibitions in honour of the Hebrew book. Ein Geb had a radio, a good gramophone, plenty of books and records. They worked hard, but they had something to show for it.

Afikim, a few miles from the Sea of Galilee, was seventeen years old when I first visited it. It had been established in 1928 and represented an investment of about £200,000. Afikim had repaid almost 60 per cent of this cost; the rest of the expenses and investments were raised by the members themselves. It had a population of about fifteen hundred; it produced wooden boxes, orange-crates, had orchards and grain-fields, and bred cattle.

Here again they took me round to the cowsheds and stables, displaying with immense pride the well-kept animals. Then I met a middle-aged, soft-spoken man called Galliel who was editor of Afikim's weekly paper, and at the same time an expert in poultry breeding. On top of all this he had a private hobby: writing books and articles on strategy, in which he had acquired a considerable reputation.

This I found perhaps one of the most striking facts about the kibbutzim—that almost everybody in them had more than one profession or skill. So people did not let themselves get into a rut. Sometimes their achievements were very varied. A musician might be a blacksmith, a sculptress a nurse, a cowhand a poet, all at the same time. Anybody could change his job if he wanted to and had the necessary ability or the will to learn. All work was on a purely voluntary basis: we were all free to come and go, though no-one was accepted without a year's probation—even Mrs Golda Meir had to serve one when she first arrived!—and a skilled specialist was expected to give reasonable notice when he wanted to leave.

In Afikim, as in many other kibbutzim, there was a special cluster of "children's houses", according to age-groups. One was for babies and I couldn't go in because it was their supper-time and their mothers were on hand to feed them. But in the others the children were just having their meal. Furniture and fixtures were all scaled to the proper height; corners were rounded off and everything was spotlessly clean. In one small house a birthday party was going on, with a tremendous cake surrounded by jam-smeared, shining faces. I thought of the children in the Polish ghettoes and I was proud of my new country where there was no fear, no anxiety; these children, as all children should be, were sturdy and healthy and happy.

But I met others in Afikim who, like myself, carried the marks of the past horrors. A group of people had come to Palestine straight from the ordeal of the concentration camps. Though they had been in Afikim for weeks (they had arrived by air, before our *Transylvania* docked), you could still sense the tenseness, the unhappy memory of suffering lurking in their eyes, betrayed by their jerky gestures, their broken speech. There was a group, seated at a separate table, that had recently arrived from Buchenwald. Galliel told me about them, how intensely shy they were at first. They would not eat in the communal dining-hall, they would hardly speak to anybody, as if their past had created an isolation which no-one else could share. But gradually they thawed out, mingled with the others, and now were having their meals with the rest of the settlers. They were being retrained in agricultural work and intended to set up their own communal village which they planned to call Buchenwald.

When I left Afikim, late at night, the great gates had to be opened by an armed sentry. He waved goodbye to me and the headlights glittered on his rifle. It was a grim reminder of the outside world, pressing against the walls of what seemed to me a happy little isle; it demanded from my people constant watchfulness, defiance, unity, in order to preserve their security and the fruit of their hard work.

32

On another trip I went to Hulata, a medium-sized fishing village on the shores of swampy Lake Hula. It looked quite poor and primitive, though the children, as everywhere else, were rosy and neatly dressed. Hulata was not yet working on a full scale, as 30 per cent of its members had joined the British Army and not all of them had been demobbed.

On this trip Dudek came with me and we had borrowed a small car. So we drove along the bottom of the valley for a while and then started to climb. It was a new, rough road, cut out of the living rock, twisting and turning so that looking back made you dizzy. Our car jolted and swerved—Dudek drove—crawling on at a snail's pace, as there were still many stones and pot-holes. As we climbed higher and higher one of the loveliest views opened to our eyes—the broad valley with the river twisting and glittering across it, the Syrian mountains on the other side, and, closer, the slopes of the hills we were going up. Black mountain goats scampered among the boulders; it was a brilliant day and you could see a great distance. Along the road there was a stony desert with practically no vegetation. Manara, the young settlement we wanted to visit, was on top of the mountain, 2700 feet above sea-level, almost on the Lebanese frontier, which curved round here and practically isolated it. It overlooked Kfar Giladi, where there had been trouble recently. Some immigrants slipped across the frontier; the police stopped them and then surrounded the settlement so that the settlers could not come to help them. The settlers resisted, there was shooting, and the whole countryside was very close to violence. Nothing serious happened after all, but Manara was almost involved in the fight.

Manara was barely three years old at that time. A young, pretty girl received us and took us round. She had joined the settlement only a year before; here she bore her baby and here she intended to bring it up.

When the first settlers came there was nothing on the site except three old Arab cisterns, weed-choked and dirty. There is no water at Manara, no spring, no rivulet. All their drinking, washing, irrigating supplies, had to come from the sky, had to be caught during the rainy season. For almost a year they had to carry every drop for an hour and a half from the nearest Arab village in the valley. Sometimes the Arabs were friendly; sometimes they stoned those who came for water. In eighteen months they built themselves two very deep and large concrete cisterns and, except for the last few weeks of the dry season, now had sufficient water for all purposes.

When I went into their simple, frugal, but very clean communal dining-hall they offered me a tin cup of water. It was the most precious thing they could give, for it was near the end of the summer and they must have been very short of it.

But water and hostile Arabs were only part of their problem. They built themselves a dozen houses—of wood, not of stone, as at this height stone would be rather damp, and cleared about two thousand dunams (almost five hundred acres) of stones. There was nothing else to do, for all they had was the stony mountain-side and most of this clearing work had to be done by hand, as no machine could do a thorough enough job. However, they did have up-to-date farming machinery for other purposes. They planted fifteen hundred fruit-trees of the hardier kind that would take kindly to the heat. Every tree needed constant individual care; their experts figured out that eighty gallons of water a year would not only keep them alive, but make them grow fast enough to gather the first crop after five years.

They planted wheat and other cereals, they built themselves a stone armoury (this was a Government condition for every settlement), and even had a few rifles in case marauding bands should attack them. The whole settlement numbered about sixty, one third of whom were women; but they were all young and there were comparatively few children. The first seven years are always the hardest, but in Manara they were extra hard. Yet no-one complained and when I joined them at their midday meal in the small, pleasant dining-hall they all seemed to be healthy and happy. And again I felt proud of my new country. I asked them about vacancies. They said they might have some next year. I said I would come back then.

134

33

I stayed at Tel Icchak for more than two years. After the trial period I was accepted as a regular member of the Hagana, the Jewish Defence Organization, and learned a good deal about its history. It was established as a protective association against Arab terrorists in the early twenties. You could join it as a teenager, for it had a first-aid branch whose task was to look after the wounded, to take food and clothes to families who had lost everything in the fighting. Many of its older members were sent abroad, to Rumania, Bulgaria, Poland, Hungary, organizing and training Jews, like those we met in Budapest. They were members of an underground army, completely devoted to their tasks, fearless and well equipped to deal with any emergency. Many of them died in the holocaust, but the organization survived even under the worst Nazi oppression.

But then came a split that caused a great deal of trouble. The Hagana had been more or less recognized by the British authorities, and even partially armed against Arab excesses. (Of course, many of the Arabs were pro-Nazi during the war.) The split was over the crucial question of defying the British or co-operating with them. There were the moderates who advocated peaceful methods, observance of the laws, while other sections demanded the return of Transjordan to Palestine, the abolition of the White Paper, and the establishment of a Jewish sovereign state, determined to fight against whoever obstructed this goal. The first such secession was by the group known as Irgun Zwai Leumi, led by David Razil, a teacher and university graduate. Razil, who was arrested at Lydda airport early in 1939, was later freed, and died in May 1940 in a battle against the Iraqi Arabs who had revolted against Great Britain under the notorious Rashid Ali. Then there was the Stern Group, which Avram Stern founded about June 1940; he was killed in February 1942. The Irgun Zwai Leumi wanted to suspend all action against the British when war broke out but the Sternists decided to go on and never really capitulated.

I met a number of men who had travelled a good deal in Eastern Europe, organizing military training for the Jews who were about to come to Palestine and were needed in the great fight to come. In some countries, including Poland, the governments did everything at that time to facilitate the departure of the Jews. Vladimir Jabotinsky actually made a pact with Colonel Beck, the Polish Foreign Secretary, that Jews would be given arms and the means for military training. Beck wanted to get rid of us, the four million Jews of Poland. And the Hagana "envoys" were sent to make the best use of the "unofficial" Polish, Rumanian, and Bulgarian help.

It took me a little time to sort it all out, and, of course, before long things were beginning to change again. But the Hagana, I learned, had stopped all kinds of violent action well before 1939; the Irgun Zwai Leumi had declared a truce only for the duration; the Stern Group, most extremist of all, never stopped fighting.

In Tel Aviv I met a man, only a few years older than myself, who had been with Avram Stern in prison; this man, whom I'd better call Isaac, was arrested in 1939 when he returned from Poland, where he had been working for the Hagana. He was released after six months, but spent most of this time together with Stern and told me about him. Avram Stern was not a violent man by disposition and training. He had been educated at Jerusalem University and graduated in sociology and economics. A scholarship took him to Italy, where he got a doctor's degree. Isaac met him briefly in September 1938 in Warsaw, where there was a world congress of the Bethar, the Jewish youth organization of the Revisionists, with Jabotinsky presiding. Stern attended it as a delegate from Palestine. Then he went home, and in August 1939 was arrested, together with four others, who later became his close associates. One of them was known as Khanokh (his real name was Strelitz), a Lithuanian-born teacher who had come to Palestine as a boy and was later deported by the British to be interned in Eritrea. The second was Aaron H, who used to be a watchman in the orange-groves and lived after the war in Tel Aviv, under police supervision. The third was Jarka Levinstein, a young student who had escaped in 1943 from Jerusalem prison and was still at large when I got to Palestine. The fourth, Chaim Lubinsky, a lawyer who was called to the Bar in Britain, gave up all political activity and settled in England. These five were kept in prison for ten months, and there Stern met David Razil, leader of the Irgun Zwai Leumi. They tried to come to some understanding, but couldn't. When Yair (that was Stern's "cover-name") came out of prison he founded his group and began his fight not only against the British and the Arabs, but even against the other Jewish organizations. In September 1940 they attacked the Anglo-Palestinian Bank in Tel Aviv and took over five thousand pounds. Then Jabotinsky died, the only man whom all the factions respected, and there was no longer a chance for the various extremist organizations to unite in peace. The conflict became sharper every day. The Sternists accused the members of Irgun Zwai Leumi of co-operating with the Palestine police. The Irgunists, like thousands of the Hagana members, volunteered for war service, but the Sternists were against enlistment: they wanted a separate Jewish army, which was, of course, impossible at that time.

Bombs and armed robberies, assassinations and ambushes, were frequent during the next eighteen months. Then, in February 1942, three young people were arrested, one of them the same Levinstein who had been together with Stern at the time of his own arrest, the second a man known as Zachariah, and the third a young teacher named Moshe Svorai. Two of them were seriously wounded. The police said that they had "resisted arrest", but one of them was shot in the armpit, a curious place in which to get a bullet, unless you have your arm raised. In any case, both police and the Jews had their own versions of this affair, just as they had of Stern's death. For five days later, on February 12th, 1942, Stern was alone in his room with the wife of the wounded Svorai, when policemen entered and shot him. The official statement said that he had resisted, but Isaac, who insisted that he knew the truth, said that he was unarmed, that they bound and shot him when he was sitting in a chair.

It was a very stupid act, for it turned the moderate Hagana and the Irgunists against the Palestine police. They said that they might become outlaws themselves from one day to another, and if they had to die they would rather die fighting. There were more arrests. The Stern Group had been small, only four or five hundred people all told. Over three hundred were put into prison, and the remaining hundred or so were considered unimportant by the police. The authorities thought that they had made the whole group harmless. But the leaders, Stern's successors, remained at large. Originally there were six in the Inner Council, but when a reward of a thousand pounds each was offered for them four gave themselves up because they considered themselves to be innocent and pleaded that they had not been active for months. They were taken to the Athlit internment camp, then sent to Eritrea. Of the remaining two the man known as Zachariah was one, the other a youngster of seventeen. These two started to organize a whole series of acts of violence as revenge for Stern's death, working with small groups of ten or twenty people. Zachariah and the youngster, Prunin, were the quarries in a country-wide hunt. In the end Zachariah was arrested about four months before I arrived in Palestine, but Prunin was still at large.

At the outbreak of the war forty-two members of the Hagana were arrested and sent to Acre (or, as we called it, Akku) prison. One of the middle-aged men at my kibbutz told me that when these men were rounded up he, as a member of the Hagana, was ordered by his organization to apply for the job of prison guard at Acre. Someone must have smoothed his path, for he was given the post, though he certainly had no qualifications for it. Within a short time he discovered that there were three other comrades of his in the group of guards. It took only a day or two before these forty-two had everything they could desire—books, newspapers, magazines; even their mail was regularly delivered to them. The Hagana needed its leaders and were determined that prison should not keep them from exercising their leadership. And the same forty-two who were locked up at Acre were the men who led the British advance into Syria when the time came to clear the Vichy and Nazi forces from that country.

34

All this I learned gradually. I was once or twice approached to join the Stern group, but each time refused. I moved to Tel Aviv in the summer of 1947, and started to work as a mechanic, which gave me access to all kinds of tools and machinery needed for our underground organization. I spent a good deal of time with my detachment of the Hagana. By that time I was experienced in the use of arms and high explosives, including dynamite. The leaders of the Hagana knew that before very long we would have to go into action, and they were looking for people who would become the N.C.O.s and officers of the future Israeli Army, no longer an illegal but a national one. I volunteered and was sent to the kibbutz Ginosar, near Lake Tiberias. There I organized a special group, instructing them in the use of dynamite and mines.

We first went into action late in December 1947. Our attack was on two radar stations and the oil pipelines near Haifa. Five days later a railway bridge near Benyamina was blown up. On the same day the Irgun people issued a statement saying that they had kept silent for a year, but now they would do so no longer. They accused the Hagana of having agreed to the blowing up of the King David Hotel (which happened in July 1946). I was much too unimportant a cog in the underground army to understand all this bickering. The British themselves knew that their time in Palestine was running out. But that did not mean that there was not a good deal of killing and maiming still to come in the remaining months. Three days after the blowing up of the Benyamina bridge three Irgun members who had been sentenced to death for their part in the attack on Acre jail almost three months earlier were executed. Irgun then announced that two British sergeants whom they had kidnapped had been tried and executed: their bodies were found hanging in a wood near Nathanya. The officer who cut them down was severely injured by a mine.

We discussed this at great length in my group and argued endlessly. We had learned by now that we couldn't depend on anybody but ourselves; but the kind of killing which had cost the lives of both British and Jews was not to our liking. If the Jewish State was to be born it could not have terror and torture for its midwives, or it would never grow up sane and healthy. When the Jewish Agency leaders and the Vaad Leumi executives, together with the mayors of Tel Aviv and Nathanya, issued a statement saying that terrorism must end because peace was an "inexorable national necessity", my friends and I felt they were right; but we didn't see how we could stop it. One thing we couldn't do was to betray our fellow-Jews, however wrong their views and actions were, to the British or to anybody else.

All through that hot summer and autumn of 1947 the struggle continued. Early in August some forty people were arrested, including the mayors of Tel Aviv and Nathanya, the very people who had advocated restraint and peaceful means. The Revisionist youth organization was declared unlawful and its property confiscated.

By now the Arabs were beginning to attack us too. In the first eight months of that year at least twenty-five Jews were killed by them, and each death provoked more fighting, more killing on both sides. There were clashes in Jaffa during which two Arabs died and the barbed-wire barricades went up between that city and Tel Aviv. Some said that the ex-Mufti of Jerusalem, who had been strongly pro-Nazi and who now lived in Cairo, was inciting the Arabs to violence. In mid-August several more deaths occurred in the area between Jaffa and Tel Aviv. Many fires were started; an Arab market and some houses were gutted. Then a detachment of the Hagana, though it was not my group, shot dead four Arabs in a house in Tel Aviv, and afterwards blew it up. Among the people who died were four children. This was done in retaliation against an Arab attack on a Jewish night-club in the same area, though the Hagana issued a statement saying they hadn't known there were any children in the house they dynamited or they wouldn't have done it. Many innocent people died in those months just because they happened to be in the wrong place at the wrong time. And all the time the United Nations Commission was talking away in Geneva, discussing whether there should be partition or federation or confederation in Palestine. Both we and the Arabs were becoming more and more impatient with their sub-committees and study groups and reports. Many thousands of Jews were waiting to come to Palestine and were prevented by the British; some were even taken back to Germany, which was the last place they wanted to go. The Jewish Agency protested that the attempts of refugees to enter Palestine were not illegal; it was the prevention by the British that was. The British Government, contrary to the United Nations Charter, tried to frustrate the determination of the Jewish people to rescue themselves.

Until I joined the Hagana and became involved in the systematic sabotage and the struggle against the Arabs I did not bother much about politics. But now I read the papers every day, I listened to the radio and discussed every new development with my friends, some of whom had been with me in Hungary and afterwards in Russian service hunting for Nazi war criminals. At the end of August the Geneva UN committee

140

issued its report. They recommended unanimously that the British mandate should end as soon as possible and that Palestine should become independent, with the transition period as short as it could be. During this time the authority that was to administer Palestine and prepare it for independence would be responsible to the United Nations. There were other points about the Holy Places, about international arrangements for helping the 250,000 European Jews in various camps and assembly centres, about the future constitution of the country, citizenship, and a call to "end the acts of violence which have far too long beset the country". There was both a majority and a minority plan with details as to how the general principles should be carried out. We liked the majority plan better, but even that did not quite satisfy us, and the Arabs did not like it at all, saying that if the United Nations accepted it they would fight it with all their strength. The Stern group called on all Jews to prepare for a long war against the British.

Three months later, on November 29th, 1947, the United Nations rejected the Arab proposal for a federal state consisting of Jewish and Arab cantons and approved partition into Jewish and Arab states and the international city of Jerusalem. Thirty-three states voted for it, thirteen against, and ten abstained. Of course, the Syrian delegate declared the decision to be "illegal and unjust".

On the same day I volunteered for the Israeli Army, the Sheruth Haam.

35

Three days later the Arabs began a protest strike. Many fires were started, with looting and fighting between the Arabs and the Jews in Jerusalem, in Jaffa, and elsewhere. The British troops had to intervene several times to save women and children. A curfew was imposed on the Arab communities. On that day I was accepted by the Army and was sent to the kibbutz Ginosar on Lake Tiberias. Just before I left, a large detachment of Arabs armed with automatic rifles and grenades fought a pitched battle with the Hagana, penetrated into Tel Aviv, and set fire to a large timber-yard. British troops were now manning

141

machine-gun posts between Jaffa and Tel Aviv. There was also fighting in Haifa and Jerusalem.

The next three months I spent partly in Ginosar and partly on various assignments for the Hagana, which had now become the Sheruth Haam. At Ginnosar I took part in a sapper course which was as concentrated as possible, for we felt we did not have very much time before large-scale and general fighting began. I had the advantage of having learned about dynamite, gelignite, detonators, and booby-traps, first during the months I had spent with Stach Babij and then during the time in Hungary when we were studying these things in preparation for going to Palestine. After the course I was made Chief Instructor of the Engineering Corps. It was a fine title, but my military rank was only sergeant, and, anyhow, in the Israeli Army there wasn't very much difference between officers and other ranks.

We worked very hard at the course, and then I travelled a good deal to the various detachments to train instructors and to give crash courses in high explosives. All this time the skirmishes with the Arabs continued. The convoys travelling from Jerusalem to Tel Aviv had their drivers armed, for in spite of police escort they were always under attack by the Arabs of Ramle and other places along the route. Sometimes they just threw stones, sometimes they used guns, and the Jewish drivers returned their fire or threw bombs. Sniping was almost constant in Tel Aviv, which periodically erupted into open clashes. By the end of the first week in December all Tel Aviv Jews between eighteen and twenty-five were asked to register at the Jewish Agency offices, and younger boys were invited to register for messenger and other auxiliary duties. Our army was getting organized and we did not lack volunteers. The goal was to enrol some 80,000 men and women into what we called a "home guard". This was now essential because the British announced that British and Arab police would be withdrawn from Tel Aviv (but not from Jaffa) and the Jewish police and "home guard" would take over their duties.

In the second and third week of December I spent some time in Jerusalem. Both sides were making attacks; every day ten or fifteen people were killed. British troops moved into the Old City. When ten Jews were killed in a Jewish convoy travelling south from Jerusalem in the Hebron area we retaliated by throwing bombs and grenades into Arab garages in Jerusalem, and one of our groups, dressed as soldiers and policemen,

142

attacked the Arab village of Ar-Tur. Day by day the fighting spread, to Haifa, to Bethlehem, to Safad in the north, to the Negeb, to Beersheba. In that fortnight after the United Nations declaration of independence we lost about a hundred civilians and members of our security forces and the Arabs about the same; hundreds were injured.

Nor did the following weeks and months bring any lessening in the conflict. More and more ships sailed from European and African ports for Palestine. Many of them were intercepted by the British and the would-be immigrants brought to Haifa, where they were trans-shipped for internment in Cyprus. (They were no longer sent back to their departure points.) But quite a few, especially the smaller ones, slipped through, like the ship called *United Nations*, which beached herself at Naharya. All the immigrants managed to escape inland. We were starting also to bring in arms and high explosives in ordinary merchant-ships, and we had to organize their collection at the ports and their transport to our various underground arsenals. Now and then our friends in America and other places slipped up: early in January, for instance, the customs people at Jersey City found that some thirty cases labelled "used machinery" really contained almost 70,000 lb of TNT. What worried them specially was that the tins were marked "U.S. Corps of Engineers". But it was not very difficult to get surplus war material if you paid cash, and very few of these cargoes were intercepted.

We also began to get some aid from the British, who were, by now, heartily sick of their doomed peace-keeping task in Palestine and would have been only too glad to leave. When Arab prisoners tried to escape from Acre jail all except one were recaptured by British troops. (A British sergeant who had taken part in this round-up was later kicked to death by the prisoners.)

Both sides used various tricks and disguises for various "actions". A group of Jews dressed as Arabs drove a lorry laden with orange-boxes that held high explosive into a narrow lane next door to the building which housed the Arab National Committee in Jaffa. They managed to escape before the explosion all but destroyed the building, the central police station next to it, a bank, and several shops. Many people were killed. It was a very daring exploit. The same group also blew up the Semiramis Hotel in Katamon, Jerusalem, which was the headquarters of Arab guerrillas and the youth organization. At least that was what *our* side said; the British denied it and were very angry with the Hagana for publicly claiming credit for the attack. The Spanish consul had died in the explosion, and that, of course, was very unfortunate. Our people said they were sorry and would do everything to see that it didn't happen again, but innocent bystanders are always likely to get hurt if they accidentally get into the line of fire. Only two days after the Semiramis affair more bombs exploded in Jerusalem outside some Arab houses, killing fifteen people; the police fired on the attackers, killing two and capturing three others. After that British police were set to guard all Government offices where both Jews and Arabs worked. The shops closed in Jerusalem for several days.

The rest of January was just as hectic and violent. The Arabs kept on attacking the kibbutzim; sometimes they were driven off by British troops, sometimes our people managed to beat them off. But every day dozens were killed. The size of the Arab bands grew; in the middle of the month more than two thousand surrounded four of our settlements between Jerusalem and Hebron. This time the Arab Higher Executive sent out some people and told them to disperse before a real, large-scale battle developed. But next day a large Hagana force which was going as reinforcement to one of the kibbutzim was attacked north of Hebron and we lost thirty-five men. It was now real war, but without proper battle-lines. The British were trying hard to keep the fighting localized, but not succeeding too well.

36

On the morning of May 14th, 1948, my commander sent for me.

"Emil," he said, "at midnight today the British mandate will end. And we will become a sovereign state."

"Yes, Colonel."

"That means we will be immediately attacked by all the Arab states. The cease-fire means nothing to them, nor can *we* keep it, for we must make ourselves secure. One of the most important things is to stop the Jordan tanks from crossing over the

144

river. The bridges must be blown up. Take a dozen men and do it. Good luck."

I picked the most experienced among those I had trained and we set out for Gesser Emek Hajarden. It was dusk by the time we reached the three bridges. Across the river we saw some clouds of dust, barely visible against the horizon.

"They're moving up, Sergeant," Jacob, one of my corporals, said.

"They're still three or four miles away," I said. "There's just time. Get going."

We scattered and moved up to the three bridges, paying out the lines, fastening the charges to the pillars and underneath the main span. We had just about finished and were getting back to the shallow ditch where we had placed the detonators when the first Jordanian tanks appeared over the slight rise of ground on the other side.

I had the central position, with Jacob and a Yemenite Jew called Shmuel on my left and right. I told them: "Wait until I give you the signal!"

We waited, tensely, as the tanks started to manœuvre parallel with the river, as if getting into position for the crossing. Now the first one began to move down to the approach of the centre bridge. It swayed and dipped like some huge animal trying to get a secure footing. I felt the sweat run into my eyes, but I was too intent on the job to wipe my forehead. Then just as the lead tank was to pass on to the bridge I gave the signal.

Down went the plungers—and up went the central bridge. There was a good deal of dust, and it took a few seconds to see that neither the left nor the right bridge had been damaged. The electric batteries must have failed—our equipment was neither as good nor as new as we would have wished—which meant that only a third of our assignment had been carried out.

The moment after the explosion the tanks began to fire, their cannon spewing flame and the machine-guns mounted on them chattering angrily. They were still not on the bridges. The central one was almost totally destroyed: two of its spans had collapsed into the river and the leading tank had been carried into the water by the explosion. I could see the crew trying to scramble out.

There was only one thing to do. "Stay here . . . cover me!" I told Jacob and Shmuel. Then, quickly snatching up some extra batteries and wire, I ran for the bridge on the left.

I could see the tanks firing, I heard the bullets whistle by, and now and then the stones around me were chipped by the impact. Jacob, Shmuel, and the rest of my group had started to fire back, but we only carried small arms and could not make much impression on the tank's armour.

It was a very long couple of minutes before I reached the bridge. Here I was reasonably safe, or so I thought until I noticed that the men from the stranded tank had managed to get out and were firing at both bridges. I worked with a speed fiercer than I had ever managed before and re-wired the charges in a few minutes. Fortunately the tank commander must have thought he was facing a much larger force and did not give the order to advance.

I now slipped into the water and made my way through the thick rushes to the bridge on the right. I tried hard to move fast and yet without disturbing the tall reeds; but, of course, I wasn't successful. The bullets were now coming thick and fast, and one ploughed a furrow down my left leg, though I barely noticed it. At last I was under the second bridge and repeated my hurried re-wiring job. Now I crawled back on the luckily sloping ground towards my detachment. The tanks were still firing and had shortened their range. Then I saw that the first three had started to rumble forward, making for the bridge on the right.

I rose for a moment and signalled to Jacob and Shmuel. I hoped they would understand my gesture. Luckily they did: they were clever boys. As I threw myself flat, cradling my head in my arms, twin explosions shattered the evening air. They were much louder and more prolonged than the first one, so the full charges must have exploded.

The firing continued, and then stopped. I raised my head. All three bridges were gone. The main crossings over the Jordan between Israel, my new country, and Transjòrdan had been destroyed. The tanks would not be able to advance before we had time to establish our lines of defence.

That evening, back in our camp, I was promoted lieutenant, a rank which I enjoyed for exactly eight days. And, what was more important, I heard the proclamation:

"We, members of the National Council representing the Jewish people in Palestine and the Zionist movement of the world, met together in solemn assembly on the day of the termination of the British mandate for Palestine, and by virtue of the natural and historic right of the Jewish people, and by resolution of the General Assembly of the United Nations, hereby proclaim the establishment of a Jewish State in Palestine to be called Israel. As from the termination of the mandate at midnight to-night and until the setting up of duly elected bodies in accordance with the Constitution to be drawn up by the Constituent Assembly not later than October 1st, 1948, the present National Council shall act as the Provisional Government of Israel. The State will be open to all Jewish immigrants, will promote the development of the country for all its inhabitants, will be based on the precepts of liberty, justice, and peace taught by the Hebrew prophets, will uphold full social and political equality for all its citizens without distinction of race, creed, or sex, and will guarantee full freedom of education and culture. . . . With trust in Almighty God, we set our hands to this declaration in the city of Tel Aviv on this Sabbath eve, the fifth day of Iyar, 5708 (according to the Jewish calendar), May 14th, 1948. . . ."

Next day there were three air attacks on Tel Aviv; one plane was shot down and the Egyptian pilot taken prisoner. The Hagana had occupied all the former British security zones in Jerusalem and was in control of all roads out of the city except the main Tel Aviv highway where the fighting was still going on. On May 16th we captured Malakir village on the Lebanese frontier and two Arab villages on the Tel Aviv–Jerusalem road. All through that week there was much bitter fighting in and around Jerusalem. Acre surrendered after seventy-two hours. We were not yet winning, but we were certainly not being defeated.

A week after we blew up the bridges my unit became part of a large detachment, which was sent to meet the invading Syrian army. After entering Samakh in the morning, where we gathered a great quantity of arms and ammunition of all kinds, we made a stand at Dagania, which was being attacked by the Syrians with tanks, armoured cars, and infantry. The battle lasted eight hours and all attacks were repulsed. When the tanks tried to break into the settlement we exploded the well-prepared tank-traps and they were destroyed. My detachment managed to capture two tanks intact when the Syrian crews surrendered.

It was the next day when our commanding officer, a Czech

147

Jew who had been promoted colonel only two weeks earlier, ordered an attack on a strongly fortified police station. It was my platoon he chose for it. I asked permission to reconnoitre. He was very nervous and curt, but in the end he agreed. So I made a circuit of the place, and when I came back I said to him, "Colonel, we must first take that hill at the back. A frontal attack would be sheer suicide.'

"Ridiculous!" he shouted. "You have enough cover to get right up to the walls. A few grenades will get those gates open. You have your orders. Just get going! You heard me, get going!"

"Colonel," I tried to argue with him, though I began to feel that it wasn't much use, "half the people in my platoon don't speak any language I speak, and I am not sure that many of the rest would understand me. I can't lead them into certain death."

He looked at me. His eyes were blazing; he really looked like a madman.

"You refuse my orders?"

"I would refuse anybody's orders if it meant massacring my own men."

"Lieutenant, I ask you for the last time, are you going to lead your platoon as I told you, or are you . . . ?"

"I'm sorry, Colonel. No."

He started to scream and rave in Czech, and, of course, I didn't understand him. Then he tore off my stars and said, "You're no longer a lieutenant, Brigg. I'll see to it that when this is over you're court-martialled, too. Now get back to your platoon! I'll show you I'm right! I'm going to lead two platoons up there and take the place in half an hour."

I said nothing, but went back to my men. A few minutes later I saw the two platoons move off with the Colonel in the lead, strutting forward like a bantam-cock. They had barely covered half the distance when the firing began. The Arabs in the police station had bazookas and a small cannon, besides machine-guns and plenty of automatics. Our men began to scatter; several were hit and killed within the first thirty seconds.

I signalled to my men and led them round the bottom of the hill, dodging from rock to rock, keeping under cover most of the way. It took us almost half an hour to make the circuit and climb the slope so that we emerged above the well-fortified, compact building. From here we could see the whole scene, spread out as if it were a panoramic picture. The Colonel and

148

his men had made very little progress: they were pinned down by murderous fire. Nor could they retreat without being wiped out. It was now mid-afternoon, blazing hot and at least five hours to darkness. Even then with a few rockets or a searchlight those in the fort could keep any frontal attack at bay.

I asked my men how many could speak Polish, Hebrew, or German. Half of them did, and I found interpreters for the others: one was a Frenchman, three were Yemenites, and six were Balts, so that I could explain to them exactly what I wanted. Of course, I had no authority any longer to give them orders, but that didn't seem to bother them. We split into three smaller groups. We used every bit of cover and moved fast. We were lucky, I suppose; we managed to get close to the walls of the police station. The Arabs had posted only two sentries on this side, and we disposed of them before they could raise the alarm. One cried out before he was clubbed insensible (I had told my men not to fire until the last moment), and we hoisted each other over the wall. At the same time the two other groups that had kept to the left and the right began to fire. In the general confusion the Arabs thought they were being attacked by a much bigger force. We were inside the fort, and after some hand-to-hand fighting we managed to take over the machine-guns and the small cannon. We blew up the cannon with a hand-grenade and turned the machine-guns on the rest of the garrison. As the mêlée became general the Colonel's detachment was no longer pinned down and they could move forward. Within an hour it was all over.

37

A few nights later I was sent with five other sappers to mine a possible crossing on the Jarmuck and stop the Jordanian infantry. We crawled within about fifty yards of the enemy positions and started our work, placing the mines. It had to be done in four stages: one person to dig the hole, the second puts in the mine, the third pays out the wire and the fourth connects the detonator while the fifth watches out for possible interruptions. We had already laid a few mines when I suddenly noticed a jackal loping in our direction. There was not a moment left

149

for hesitation or thought. I knew that the second it stepped on the wire, we would all be blown to smithereens. It was impossible to shoot the jackal for that would have betrayed our presence to the Arabs. I signalled to the boys to throw themselves on the ground—while I covered the mine with my body. I knew that the only chance of saving ourselves was to do this —for by pressing on the mine with my body I provoked the first, weak explosion which would make the mine rise about a yard high. By preventing the mine rising to this height, I could stop the second, actual explosion. There was, of course, the risk that my body would not be enough to keep the mine lower than about three feet—but we were lucky. I felt a tremendous blow against my chest which broke two of my ribs—but the mine did not explode. My comrades picked me up and dragged me back to our position. I was bandaged and within a week I was back with my unit.

By early June a truce had been arranged. Our new army hadn't done too badly. True, we had lost the Old City of Jerusalem, but almost two hundred Arab villages were in our hands. Jaffa, Haifa, Tiberias, Safad, and Jenin had been deserted by their Arab populations, and almost all the modern part of Jerusalem was held by us. I was there when, on June 16th, the commanders of the Arab forces and of the Hagana in Jerusalem, signed the map on which they had agreed, which showed the position each side had reached at the time of the cease-fire. A week later we were beginning to have trouble with the Irgun people; they had tried to bring ashore some military equipment at Tel Aviv from a ship beached on the coast. The Hagana blew up the ship offshore; there was fighting and about fifteen people were killed; sad enough, Jews killing Jews, but the new Government said it had no choice, it could not tolerate "military or political anarchy". They ended the arrangement under which members of the Irgun and the Stern Group served in the Army under their own commanders; an amnesty was offered to those who would re-enlist as regular soldiers. The truce was being broken now and again, though these were not very serious incidents. And on June 30th, we watched the last British troops leaving our country; Jewish police took over the port of Haifa.

When the truce ended on July 9th, our unit of the Golani Brigade moved from the Jordan Valley (Emek Hajarden) into Lower Galilee (Galil Hatachton), to the village of Sedgera,

150

which was Ben Gurion's home. Sedgera was about ten miles from Nazareth and about two miles from another village called Lubia. It was an important strategic point because it was at the crossroads between Lake Galilee (Kinneret), the Jordan and Galilee. Some local Arabs and the troops of Kaudgi were fighing there, having mounted several attacks against us with artillery and machine-guns.

One morning their infantry moved forward under the cover of Bren carriers and flame-throwers. Their attack drove our units back. My commander, Colonel Icchak Broschi, gave me orders to mine the terrain in front of our trenches because he foresaw new attacks. We were under strong fire as we laid our anti-tank and anti-personnel mines.

The attack was mounted before long. It was thrown back with heavy losses. We suffered less though a shell landed on the bunker of the command post and killed three officers. Next day, before sunrise, I went again forward to lay more mines when a few Bren carriers moved forward towards our trenches. One of them was blown up by a mine and the soldiers who had ridden in it turned to flee while the other carrier covered them with machine-gun fire. I crawled up to it and threw a smoke-grenade into the Bren carrier. The soldiers thought they had suffered a direct hit, scrambled out and began to run away. I jumped on the vehicle and drove the Bren carrier back to our lines. Later I went back to the first carrier which had run on the mine. Half the tracks were broken. I thought I could also drive it back to our positions but the Arabs began to fire and I realized it would be impossible to cover the open space. So I put some dynamite into the damaged carrier and blew it up.

A week later the Hagana occupied the King David Hotel in Jerusalem, and by next day the fighting was renewed everywhere. We took Lydda airport, Lydda, and Ramle in a large-scale attack. We had planes now and tanks and began to push on towards Latrun. The fiercest fighting was around Deir Terif, and at Beit Naballah. By July 15th we were advancing on Nazareth. There were still arguments with Irgun and the Stern Group, who said they would look on any foreign troops, American, Belgian, French, or any others, as invaders even if they came as a United Nations army to enforce a partition or internationalization of Jerusalem. Another truce was signed twelve days after the new fighting began.

In Jerusalem the Hagana arrested, put on trial, and executed a Jewish official of the Electric Corporation. He was found guilty of espionage for the Arab Legion. I remembered Janikowski when I heard about it. I did not know the man, I only knew he had been a major in the Royal Engineers during the war. I wasn't sorry for him, for I was certain he had been guilty of betraying his own people, but I wished we had waited with his execution until the war was over and there was less passion and less hate. Five others, all British subjects, held under the same charges were formally charged with espionage, but were remanded for two weeks; one of them was even released on bail. The truce was prolonged, but our people did not like this; we wanted a proper peace treaty or at least the start of negotiations. (Today, as I am writing this, there is still no peace between Israel and the Arabs. A friend of mine once said that there was nothing as permanent as the temporary.) We felt we had won the war, and we were not going to be dictated to by anybody. The Army made a deal with Irgun Zwai Leumi, who were allowed to keep their independent formations but would co-ordinate their activities with those of the Regular Army, in which I was serving. This made things a little easier. And we began to make arrangements for getting more than half a million European Jews to Israel. Many thousands had already arrived since the mandate ended, and now a plan to bring in at least ten thousand a month was prepared; ships and reception areas were all made ready. We needed men to grow crops, to irrigate the land, and above all to fight until what we had won was safe. There were 800,000 Jews in the Moslem countries and they had to be rescued before there was another holocaust, another series of massacres and pogroms.

The truce was broken again and again, especially in and around Jerusalem, sometimes with quite heavy shelling, sometimes by sporadic fighting; then it was patched up once more for a few days or even a week or two. Our Government, having persuaded the Irgun to merge with the Regular Army, tried to liquidate the Stern Group to prevent irresponsible terrorist acts. Early in September one of their camps was surrounded and fifteen of the Stern Group arrested. Then, on September 17th, four members of the Hazit Hamoledth, a group that was part of the Sternists but extremist even by their standards, murdered Count Bernadotte, the United Nations mediator, and Colonel Serot, an observer on his staff, as they were driving

152

through Katamon, a quarter of Jerusalem held by our side. The Hazit Hamoledth quite openly claimed "credit" for the killings. They were senseless, stupid murders and they did us Jews a great deal of harm. We in the Army certainly agreed with our Foreign Minister, Moshe Shertok, who spoke of an "abominable assassination" by "desperadoes and outlaws". Three days after the murders emergency regulations were issued for the prevention of terrorism; heavy sentences of imprisonment were to be given for taking part in such acts, and even for membership or support of the terrorist organizations. Almost two hundred members of the Stern Group were arrested in Jerusalem, and scores more in Tel Aviv; by the end of the month Nathan Yellin, the leader of the Group, and Matatiahu Shmulevitz, its operations commander, were also caught in Haifa. But on October 9th the guards at Jaffa jail were overpowered by some Sternists and over a hundred prisoners escaped. Eighty remained on the spot, but outside the prison, and told journalists that they "just wanted to prove that there are no walls which can hold us". At the end of the day some forty men were unaccounted for; a hundred and fifty were moved to Acre prison.

A week later our regiment was sent south to the Negeb. The situation had worsened there. The UN had ordered a cease-fire, but our side said we wouldn't suspend operations until we had full guarantees that our traffic would pass unmolested by the Egyptians and further attacks would stop. The Egyptians replied that *they* would stop when we had moved back to our original positions.

On October 17th we mounted a raid on Arab positions while our planes were attacking the airfields at El Arish, in Sinai, and at Gaza, and the troop concentrations around Majdal and Daluja. The air attacks were a sort of "softening-up", and it was a wonderful feeling that we had our own planes, our own pilots —that, as an army, we had "grown up". By October 19th we had surrounded Gaza and Majdal and the motorized columns of which my detachment was part attacked the Egyptian convoys between Beit Jibrin and Bethlehem. Two days later we had occupied Beersheba and the village of Beit Wettif. We found that the Egyptians were much easier to deal with than the Arab Legion: they never put up a prolonged fight and their officers were neither very brave nor very clever. A cease-fire was to begin in the afternoon of October 22nd, but during the morning we threw in everything we had around Majdal and Faluja and the approaches to Bethlehem and captured a village north of Gaza. The whole of the Negeb, except for Gaza and a few small pockets, was in our hands; we felt that the Egyptian resistance had pretty well crumbled. So we very properly refused to move back to whatever positions we had held before the offensive started on October 15th. Our Prime Minister, Ben Gurion, declared quite bluntly that we would never withdraw from the Negeb, which we needed for our immigrants and which we would turn into the "garden of Israel". Not that there was much of a garden about it in those days. The Egyptians withdrew from Isdud because they had no water and no food; we moved in and promptly had to start feeding the Arab civilians, who were completely destitute.

At the end of the month we were moved again, to attack both sides of the Arab salient in Galilee, at Tarshiha in the west and Josh in the east. Our two columns met at a place called Sa'sa, and here we fought a final battle which drove the Arab forces under Fawzi Kaukji across the Lebanese frontier. For the first time Palestinian Arabs fought on our side—some Druse cavalry, who did remarkably well. We killed or captured almost a thousand of the enemy. There were only three Arab forces left as effective opponents for us: the Syrians, who had a small bridgehead at Mishmar Hay Yarden, south of Lake Hula; the Iraquis in the area of Nablus, Tulkarm, and Jenin; and, of course, the Arab Legion.

Before that first half-year of our independence ended we took Majdal in the Negeb, held on to Beersheba, bottled up some three thousand Egyptians in the Faluja pocket, fought our way through to the sea in the south, and on the very last day of 1948 captured two villages close to the Egyptian border and routed a brigade based in this area. Early in the New Year we even pursued them fairly deep into Egyptian territory, reached some airfields, and, after inflicting considerable damage, returned to what we now considered Israeli territory. Except for the Old Town of Jerusalem, we had pretty well gained all the land we wanted. There was still some isolated fighting to be done, and a good deal of talking, with which we soldiers were little concerned. But at the end of May I was discharged from the Army, though later I was called back again for a few weeks. I had again risen to the rank of sergeant, though my insubordination during that attack on the police station was still held against

154

me and I was not promoted to officer's rank. But on the day before I left the Army I was called to my C.O.'s office. There were about half a dozen high-ranking officers, including two generals, present. It was my brigade commander who told me that I had been awarded the Gibor Israel. He also told me that I was the sixth person to be given the highest military decoration of our country, and that only one other of the six, another sergeant, was alive: the other four had won the award posthumously. Later another six awards were given, but altogether there are only seven of us alive who are entitled to wear the decoration.

38

I was now a civilian and I had to make a living. For a while I worked for the municipal government of Tel Aviv, supervising the demolition work along the seashore, where a good many rocks and cliffs had to be blown up to enable us to build a coast-road, to expand the existing beaches, and to create a deep-water harbour. It was hard work and it had an element of risk, which I enjoyed.

But it was interrupted by my second call-up, and when I came back again, after a few weeks, I was at a loose end. There was an uneasiness in me; I knew I was missing something, but I couldn't put a name to it, however hard I tried. I took occasional jobs, driving, repairing cars, whatever gave me enough money to live on. And a good deal of the money I made I spent on drink. I had never liked alcohol very much, and I didn't like it now, except that it made me forget my restlessness and loneliness. I found that I couldn't bear crowds, that I was shrinking from talking to anybody except a very few old friends. And even those I began to neglect and avoid. When we met, rarely, I soon got into an argument over some small, ridiculous point, and ended up shouting at them.

Then my friend Simon came to Tel Aviv on leave and tracked me down, for I had been changing my room constantly, seldom staying in the same place for more than a week. But Simon, who was a major in the Air Force, in charge of ground defence and anti-aircraft batteries at one of our advanced fields, was a persistent man. When he found me I was drunk. He picked me up and put me in his car. He drove me down the seashore and forced me to take a swim. It was late September and the water was pretty cold. I didn't want to, but he stripped and dragged me in. We fought and he knocked me out. I fell into the water and swallowed quite a large dose of the Mediterranean. I came up spluttering and found Simon laughing at me. So I began to laugh, too. After that it was easier.

We went into a restaurant—I hadn't been eating very much for the past few weeks—and we began to talk. I told Simon about Poland and about our journey into Hungary; about the early, pleasant days in Mohács, and then the not so pleasant weeks in the cellar of the police station and the prison, where all those experts had tried so hard to make us speak. I wondered what had happened to the blue-eyed Silesian Gestapo man who was so inventive about torture.

"And what happened to all the others?" Simon said. "I don't believe that one in ten of those bastards got his just deserts."

"You think they'll get off scot-free?"

"Some of the worst mass murderers escaped from Germany," Simon said. "Eichmann. Dr Mengele. The doctors who killed hundreds of people at Dachau with their crazy experiments. Bormann—he may still be alive. There's a list as long as my arm with only the most notorious on them."

"But if they have escaped . . ."

"Not all of them. There were so many; the majority just stayed put, forged papers, got some witnesses whom they bribed or blackmailed into clearing them. They're doing well, most of them, sometimes in the same places where they committed their crimes."

"You mean they changed their names?"

"Not necessarily. They have friends in the regional offices, the ministries, the police headquarters. So many papers have been destroyed or lost, and with a little help you can make evidence disappear even when it has been preserved. And if they are in danger they are warned, so they can move . . ."

He went on to tell me about the various underground Nazi organizations, some of which had been set up well before the end of the war when the SS and Gestapo men felt that the day of defeat was approaching, the noose was tightening around their necks. He spoke of a man called Velasco, a Nazi agent in Spain, who had helped to establish contact with the pro-Nazi

156

Perón regime of Argentina; with his aid and that of Germans living or born in South America, huge quantities of gold, works of art, valuable patents and documents, were sent overseas, first through France and then later by air to Majorca, from which point German submarines transported them to Argentina. They called this Operation Tierra del Fuego. At the same time they opened bank accounts in Switzerland, Liechtenstein, Spain, and Latin America, established holding companies with "straw-men" fronting for them. Then there was the organization called *Die Schleuse* (Sluice or Dam) which began its operations in May 1945, and by 1948 had helped some three thousand Nazis to escape. One of the main routes, our agents had established, led through Schleswig-Holstein to Denmark, and then to South America; another to Bari and the Middle East. The most important was the Genoa and Naples route via Innsbruck. There was a cover organization called *Evangelisches Hilfswerk* which supplied the necessary papers cheaply and provided the contacts in South America. A whole spider's web covered Italy, Spain, and the Latin American states, which is why the present escape system was called *Die Spinne* (The Spider); this, Simon said, had begun to function only about a year earlier. Other networks included *Odessa* for former SS officers and the *Stille Hilfe* (Silent Help). There were now whole Nazi colonies in Paraguay and Brazil.

The more Simon spoke the more depressed I became and in the end I asked him to stop. He was surprised, but did not insist. We did not meet for a couple of days. I was still drinking, though less than before, and I kept on brooding about what Simon had said. Then he came on leave again, bringing with him his friend Reuben, a captain in the Air Force whom I had known before we came to what was then still Palestine. He was the youngest among us, only twenty-one. Simon was twenty-three, and I was the senior, though, of course, I was only a sergeant. My friends didn't pull their rank on me: I would have soon punched them on the nose if they had.

We went out to eat in one of the open-air restaurants in Ramat Gan, and then took a long walk. We talked about girls and whether there would be more fighting before long. And then I said, I don't quite know why, "We ought to go to Germany."

"Whatever for?" Reuben asked. "Didn't you have enough of the *Herrenvolk?*"

"I have thought a great deal about what you told me, Simon," I went on. "We can't stop *all* those bastards getting away and living in luxury . . . but we could stop a few."

"Stop them?" Reuben sounded puzzled.

"Execute them."

"You're crazy," Reuben said.

"Shut up, Reuben!" Simon sounded quite serious. "Let's hear what Emil has on his mind."

"Track down a few, a couple of dozen, maybe, and make sure they pay for what they did to our people."

"Just like that? But there have been trials, there are courts."

"Sure. How many people did they try at Nuremberg? For every one that got his deserts—you said so yourself—there are hundreds on the loose. I don't think I can ever resign myself to an ordinary, humdrum life if I don't do something to settle accounts—at least a small part of them. I keep thinking of it day and night. It's like an ulcer eating away at my guts. I thought I wouldn't need to explain it to you—you went through the same things, you lost your families."

There was a short silence. I sat down on a piece of broken masonry at the roadside. Reuben sat down beside me. Simon remained standing.

"It's too late, Emil," Reuben said. He had now realized, I think, that I was serious. "The time's over for partisans, for unofficial executioners. There are people whose job it is to deal with those bastards. And the Germans themselves have been putting some of them on trial. Let's leave it to them."

"No." It was Simon who spoke up. "I think Emil is right. Mind you, I don't know how we are going to find them. We can't just walk up to somebody and say, 'Excuse me, did you kill any Jews?' and shoot him. Or pick names from the telephone-book."

Reuben shook his head. "You're arguing with yourselves, both of you, and you won't get anywhere. I say, forget it. Didn't God say, 'Vengeance is mine'?"

"Maybe, but sometimes He forgets. He must be too busy." I knew I sounded bitter, but I couldn't help it. "And that bit about God's mills being slow but grinding exceeding small, well, I don't think we should wait until He gets around to it."

We talked all night; first, sitting there at the roadside, then in a café, and finally in my room. We did not get anywhere. Reuben was still practical, and now Simon was beginning to take his side, saying that we'd better leave it to the police and the courts. There were too many difficulties. And if we killed the wrong man, how would we feel about it, how could we square it with our consciences? I felt alone, more solitary than ever because I didn't agree with either of them. I had no answers to their objections, I wasn't as clever or as articulate as they were: they had had a better education than I. But I knew, deep down, that I would never have peace, never lead a normal life, until I had done something to purge myself of the anger and grief that had been festering in me for more than eight years, for a third of my entire life.

39

A week or so later Simon found me again. I had moved once more; I had lost my sixth or seventh job because I was late every morning, and I was drinking more than before, though when he came I happened to be half sober.

"I had a letter from David," he said.

"Yes?" I wasn't very interested. David had been in our group at Mohács. He was one of those who had managed to get away when Olek, Danuta, and I were arrested, and he went underground, continuing to do very important intelligence work until the Russians arrived. Later, in January 1945, I met him in Vienna. He hadn't come to Palestine, or if he had I had missed him.

"I think he can help us."

I sat up. I had a splitting headache, but I was interested.

"Help?"

"He's still in Vienna. He's studying economics."

"That must be nice," I said dully.

"But he's also doing some work for our people. For the trackers. Unofficially, of course. I'm going to write to him. Maybe he can get us the information we need. A list of names. The rest will be up to us. Or maybe David will join us if he hasn't got anything more important to do."

"Have you told Reuben?"

"Yes. He's willing to come with us."

I jumped up and embraced Simon. I even performed a little dance. It was as if someone had given me an unexpected present of which I had dreamt a long time, but never believed I would get.

But it wasn't so simple or quick as we thought. First David wrote that he was going away on some mission to Italy and wouldn't be back before late September or October. And, of course, we couldn't put into a letter what we wanted exactly, nor could he tell us much by post. Letters from Austria were censored: there was still a four-power occupation, and we all had to be careful.

Then there was the question of money. We agreed that we must not ask any official or semi-official body to finance our trip. Not even if we pretended that it was something entirely different, like seeing about compensation which would have been due to all of us from the German authorities. (When the time came for me to apply I refused to sign the papers. I did not want any of their blood-money.) So we put what we had together, Simon, Reuben, and I. I had kept some savings apart, as a kind of iron reserve, and I sold a few things I still had left. Also I went to work while we were waiting for the arrangements to be completed—passports and tickets and foreign currency, all of which needed permits and involved a lot of red tape. I worked for two months, harder than ever before, doing a good deal of overtime, and I had a nice little nest-egg at the end of it.

Then, in the last week of October, the three of us took a Sabena plane to Brussels.

It was cold in Belgium, especially cold for us because we had been used to the hot climate of Israel, and the heavy clothes we had to wear were uncomfortable at first. It was raining a good deal. But the lights were on and there was plenty of food in the shops, and good beer and wine. It was the first time in my life that I had seen a West European capital and I gaped like a yokel, for there was so much to see. The world had changed immensely since my boyhood in Poland, and even there I had seen only Cracow and Lwow for short visits before the Germans came and turned the whole country into a drab, deadly prison camp.

The Belgians were having some trouble with their King, who had surrendered to the Germans in 1940; they were about to hold a plebiscite to decide whether he should be allowed to come back and occupy the throne again. Though the country looked prosperous and rich, we were told that there was plenty of unemployment and foreign labour would not be admitted until things got better. We stayed with a distant relative of Simon's, a professor who was teaching at Brussels University. We spent two weeks in his apartment and he was very kind to us. We did not tell him why we had come to Europe. We were waiting to hear from David whether we should go to Vienna or meet him somewhere else. We weren't quite sure where we should start our operations. We wanted to pick a city or a province where there was the biggest concentration of ex-Nazis, where we could do our work quickly and then move on.

We also had to get arms. We did not bring any guns with us because we did not know whether we would be searched either before we left or by the Belgian customs. But a few days after our arrival Simon found out that it was easy to buy revolvers and even sub-machine-guns in Belgium. After the war there were so many about they could be had dirt-cheap. And ammunition too. We could pick and choose, and each of us selected his favourite weapon. I got a Smith and Wesson, Reuben a Lüger, and Simon a Colt. We also had one machine-pistol.

Every evening after the professor and his family had gone to bed we kept on arguing how we should act. We agreed that we must be absolutely sure that the people we tracked down deserved their fate. We intended to kidnap them, force them to sign confessions, and then turn them over to the German authorities for trial. At least that was what we originally intended. But as we kept on talking about it I said, "What if they do what the Russians did in Nagykanizsa? What if they simply let them go, or free them on bail? They'll certainly do everything to get the hell out of Germany before they can be tried."

"Maybe if we handed them over to the French or the Americans," Reuben suggested.

"And what would happen to us if we did that?" I argued. "You expect a medal or at least a pat on the back? We'd soon land in jail, for kidnapping or interfering with the course of justice!"

I couldn't quite keep the bitterness out of my voice.

"Emil's right," Simon said, a little reluctantly. "We have to make absolutely sure we're after the people who deserve to be judged, and then carry out the sentence ourselves."

"Yes, I suppose that's what we'll have to do," Reuben agreed, somewhat to my surprise. "I'd hate to go back to Israel after being on a fool's errand."

41

Three days later we heard from David and left for Vienna. He met us at Schwechat, the airport, and took us to his two-room apartment not far from the Stefansdom, the big cathedral that was still being repaired. Vienna had suffered a great deal more damage than Brussels and was something of a mess; it was difficult to tell what was being torn down and what was being built. The country was still under four-power occupation, though the Austrians were beginning to agitate for all the occupying forces to leave. (It would take another six years before the Russians agreed.) There were still many Nazis at large; on the day we arrived six men had been arrested in Upper Austria for carrying on underground activities. The Russians were making loud protests about a Fascist revival, saying that no real denazification had been carried out in the Western zones, and they demanded that Austria should pay for the repatriation of prisoners-of-war from the Soviet Union, which meant, as the country was broke, that the Americans and the British would have to pay.

David was glad to see us, and introduced us to his colleague, Aaron—that was his "operating name". Aaron's official job was to arrange for the transfer of Jews from Poland to Israel via Austria. At that time it was a large-scale operation: big camps were established for them (most of them were young), and after they were medically examined and properly registered they were sent on to Italy and from there to Israel. Though the Russians were still friendly enough towards our young state, emigration was very difficult from the Communist countries. Our people were being smuggled out in groups of ten and twenty; the Austrians did not raise any objection as long as it was understood that none of them would try to stay there.

This was important work, but both Aaron and David were also concerned with tracking down German and Austrian war criminals. When they managed to find one they handed him over to the American authorities and he was tried by the appropriate military or civilian courts.

We offered to help them, and David said that there was one particular mission where he could do with some help. The most important quarry of all the Jewish investigators at that time was Adolf Eichmann. I had already heard about him from my Russian colonel and from the few surviving Hungarian Jews I had met in Budapest. Eichmann had spent quite a long time in Budapest, where he was supposed to have beaten a young Jewish boy to death, though his main job had been to organize the mass deportation of the Hungarian Jews, of whom fewer than 10 per cent survived.

The trouble was that though many people had seen him and had even talked to him, for he had actually negotiated the exchange of some Jews for lorries and for gold, there seemed to be no photographs of him. Mere descriptions were no use: they varied, and in any case he could easily have grown a beard or shaved his head. A photograph was essential if a large-scale organized hunt was to succeed. There were certain facial characteristics that could not be hidden—for instance, the shape of the ears—and we had our experts who would provide the necessary references for our "hunters".

Now, David had discovered that one of Eichmann's mistresses (he apparently had had one in every country where he had operated for any length of time) was living in Vienna, or, rather, just outside the capital. He got his information from Aaron, who in turn had got it from one of Eichmann's former aides. This aide had carried little presents to the lady, who was now in her late twenties and still very pretty.

David did not look Jewish at all: he was also quite handsome. He decided to seduce the lady. But at the same time he wasn't certain whether Eichmann or his friends were keeping an eye on her; maybe they were even thinking of helping her to move from Austria to reunite her with her lover. So he needed a bodyguard, or, rather, in case it should become noticeable, several who could take turns in following him discreetly, keeping an eye on the house in which the girl lived while he was visiting her. He had gone to considerable trouble to discover that she frequented one particular cinema and one small pastry-shop, and he spent several weeks just "dropping in" at these places before he tried to speak to her. At first she was rather stand-offish, but that changed quickly enough, for she was lonely and also resentful, probably because her lover hadn't yet sent for her as he must have promised.

So we followed David at a little distance, Simon or Reuben or I, taking care not to appear to be shadowing him. Again, at first the lady wouldn't invite him to her apartment, and they always met at the pastry-shop. But he played her skilfully, as an angler plays a trout, and he was a good-looking boy, about two or three years older than I was, and quite an experienced ladies' man. So after a month (this happened about the time we got to Vienna) she asked him in for a cup of coffee, and then it was all plain sailing. In another three days they had gone to bed together: she was quite an attractive woman and David found an ironic pleasure in sleeping with Eichmann's former girl-friend.

He soon discovered that she hadn't the faintest idea where Eichmann was, but expected to hear from him. (She never did.) One day she showed him a photo album—the usual collection of awful snapshots of fat old ladies and men in *Lederhosen*— and David responded with polite but not excessive interest. It was the girl who pointed at one particular photo and said, "That's Adolf . . . he was my regular boy-friend."

"Well, I hope he never comes back to claim you!" David said, showing a bit of jealousy, as was expected of him, and wondering how on earth he could get hold of the picture. It was no use taking it out of the album, for he meant to keep in touch with the woman until Eichmann contacted her, if he ever did, and he did not want to make her suspicious. He told us about it, and Simon, who had the proper connections, managed to get one of those miniature cameras the Americans had developed during the war.

And so we got the picture, or, rather, David did, for we only provided a guard for him. It was the very first photograph anybody had managed to find of Eichmann; later, at his trial in Jerusalem, it was produced as the first and practically only one in existence for his identification.

Shortly after David managed to photograph it—it came out very well—he was accosted by two men when he approached the girl-friend's house. It was my turn to act as his bodyguard, and I moved up as the men tried to push David off the pave-

164

ment, towards a car. When they saw me they hurried away. Perhaps they had been ready to kidnap David, take him away, and question him, but they did not want any scandal or violence. Not long afterwards David was sent on a special job to Styria and he gave up cultivating the forsaken mistress.

42

We were getting tired of Vienna. Early in the new year we thought of moving to Linz, because the police had discovered a secret store of arms and explosives there which belonged to an underground Nazi organization formed about a year before by a former SS officer who had escaped from Germany. We thought that would be a good hunting-ground. But then Simon had another idea which attracted us more.

"Let's go to Berlin," he said one frosty morning.

Reuben scowled. "That awful city! Why?"

"You've heard of Spandau prison, haven't you?" Simon asked.

"Yes. That's where all the Nazi bigwigs are, isn't it?"

Simon nodded. "It's in the Western part of the city. It shouldn't be too difficult to get near it."

"Don't tell me you want to break into Spandau!" I protested. "Those prisoners are the best guarded in the world. We would never get near them."

"Prisoners are not always in their cells," Simon said.

Reuben looked at us. "What *are* you two talking about?" he demanded.

"About Hess. And Baldur von Schirach, the former Reich Youth Leader," Simon replied. "Not to mention Albert Speer, who was responsible for all the slave labour during the war. Raeder and Doenitz, the admirals. Funk and Neurath. A nice bunch of thugs. All penned up—for us."

"If we had a couple of telescopic rifles . . ." I said.

"Why not a howitzer?" Reuben was still unconvinced. "Maybe they'll let us drive a tank right up to the gate. I think you're both crazy."

He was still saying the same when we left for Berlin.

Before David went to Styria he and Aaron had given us some

addresses. We did not tell them, by the way, what we planned to do, though later Simon sent a report to Aaron. We had, however, discussed with both of our Vienna friends the position of the prisoners at Spandau. They were extremely well guarded, the four occupation forces taking turns to provide the guards— at least twenty people for each prisoner. Nobody seemed to think that anyone would try to get at them—certainly not the Jews, though there were some fears and rumours that the ex-Nazis still at large would make a rescue attempt. (There never was one. And in the next twenty years the prisoners either were released or died, one by one, until only Hess is left in what must be the costliest and most elaborate one-man jail in the world.)

We took a train from Vienna to Frankfurt, and then flew into Berlin, as we did not want to risk going through Russian controls. We arrived at Tempelhof and were met by a member of Aaron's organization, a young Pole who had been sent to Germany as a slave labourer and remained there after the war to work for the group tracking down war criminals.

Berlin still looked pretty horrible; I must admit that it gave us a feeling of satisfaction to see what devastation the Nazis had brought upon themselves. The Russians were making things difficult for the West, holding up traffic from Western Germany into the city; their excuse was that they wanted to smash the "wild black-marketeering rings". Lots of lorries were either held up or confiscated at the check-points; it was a cat-and-mouse game. People were being kidnapped, and the Soviet authorities were building up the East German Communist regime's authority, handing over more and more of the administrative functions. We stayed in the Gattstrasse in the Zehlendorf district, which was in the American zone. We roamed the city, spending days reconnoitring the approaches to Spandau and trying to find out all we could about the routine of changing guards, of the prisoners' exercise time, and other details. Nothing we learned got us any closer to our goal, and we were getting rather disheartened.

Then Janek, the young Pole who had met us at Tempelhof, asked us whether we wanted to see a film studio which was owned by another Pole. I wasn't very keen, but Simon and Reuben were getting bored with walking the streets and not talking to anybody except our little group. So we went to the studio, which was just a large garage full of holes, very cold,

166

very primitive; but they were making pictures and the proprietor was certainly making money. He had changed his Polish name, which nobody could pronounce, and called himself Arthur B. He spoke German with a strong Polish accent.

After we had watched the filming for a while there was a lunch break, and we had sausages and beer. Even the stars had only an extra pair of *Bockwurst*, and maybe a little scoop of potato salad on top. Mr B was a thrifty man. Simon talked to him and found out that they came from the same district in Poland. B had been in a concentration camp, and he started to trade almost as soon as he was released—just in a pair of pants and a ragged shirt. Now he was on the way to becoming a millionaire.

All this was not particularly interesting to us, but a little later Simon came over to Reuben and me and said, "Boys, you'd never guess what I've found out! Mr B has just bought a former tannery which he is going to turn into a big film studio as soon as he can get the building permit. It's only a shell now, but he says it has great possibilities. . . ."

"For whom?" asked Reuben. Then he answered his own question: "For him, I'm sure. What's a derelict tannery got to do with us?"

Simon smiled. "Not the tannery, Reuben. Its location. It happens to be exactly across the road from Spandau prison. The inside's burnt out, but part of the roof's still intact."

We both stared at him, incredulous. Then Reuben whistled. "Phew! That *is* quite a coincidence!"

"But we couldn't possibly tell B that we . . ." I started. "I mean, he would never agree."

"We don't have to tell him," Simon said patiently. "We'll just visit the place, and then ask him whether we could spend a little time on the roof to photograph the prisoners when they have their exercise. I told him we worked for an English picture agency and would also do a story about his studio and his plans."

"And if we do it," I was still doubtful, "won't he get into trouble?"

"No, of course not. If we are caught we will say that we got into the building without anybody knowing, without permission. It's a ruined one and they won't start work on it until the spring; just because he owns it doesn't make him responsible for trespassers."

I still felt we weren't being quite fair to Mr B, but I realized that Simon was right: this was a chance we couldn't miss. Next day we climbed to the roof of the burnt-out tannery. It was a hair-rising climb, worse than going up a mountain-side; any moment we thought something would crumble and we'd plummet down eight storeys. But we managed to get to the top. Quite a large part of the roof was intact, and there was enough rubble and rubbish up there, an empty water-tank, various bits of rusty machinery, to provide us with cover. And we could see the whole area of the prison spread out below us, neat and clear, like a model.

We spent three hours there the first time, until it became too dark to see anything. We had arrived too late to witness the exercise period; that would be, as we later discovered, before lunch, so that the VIPs could work up a proper appetite, I suppose. They did not have to move in a circle like we did in Pécs prison: the guards just let them out and they could sit or walk and talk to one another, though few of them did. They seemed to hate each other, or at least they weren't on speaking terms, except maybe one or two.

On the second and third days we fixed ourselves more comfortably on the roof. We found that part of an inner staircase had survived and we fastened a rope-ladder to a girder that connected with the top of it. It was still a pretty exhausting climb, but it was quicker and much safer. We carried up food and drink and cigarettes, and built ourselves a little shelter from bricks and planks. "Home from home," Reuben said. "I never thought we'd help to solve the housing problem of Berlin!"

More important than any of these preparations was the problem of the guns. We had to have telescopic rifles—two at least, because we had worked out that we wouldn't get the chance of a second shot, that both Reuben and I (we were the marksmen) had to hit our targets first time.

We asked Janek, but he couldn't help us. It was very frustrating. There we were, having a front-row view of those men, studying their every movement through binoculars, taking photographs (this was my special hobby, and I was getting to be pretty good at it), and yet they might have been behind armour plate for all we could do about picking them off! We had now plotted their exact schedule—the time they were taken for their exercise, when they went back to their cells, the

168

changing of the guards. We had decided that if possible we would choose a period when the British were supplying the guards, just to repay a little of what we felt we owed them for making life so hard for all the "illegal" immigrants.

Then Reuben met a girl who was working as a civilian at one of the many American military offices. Like David, Reuben was quite a lady-killer. The girl (a Canadian) did not have any rifles to sell, nor could she get any herself, but she knew a sergeant who was in business for himself, building up a little capital for his return to civilian life. He had a "buddy" who was in charge of the Grunewald depot, where the arms confiscated from civilians were collected and kept. (All Germans had to give up their hunting and other guns, and for several years no permits were given to civilians.) Janek had ample funds from our organization, and though the price was high because a number of go-betweens had to be paid off, a week later we did have two fine telescopic rifles with plenty of ammunition.

It was now early March, though little sign of spring showed in the battered city. We decided to prepare everything for our speedy departure, with air tickets on different flights, and then wait for a sunny day to carry out our self-chosen mission. Simon was our liaison man with Aaron's Berlin office. Reuben and I had practised our aiming dozens of times. We were certain we wouldn't miss. Even if we did not get them all, three or four would be quite an achievement. And we had ample cover up on the tannery roof: we had a very good chance of getting away long before we were spotted. We would bury the rifles in the rubble and cover all our traces.

At last the sun shone and we were in our places a good hour before the time for the Spandau prisoners' exercise. We waited for Simon, who had gone to fetch our airline tickets and make the final arrangements. Both Reuben and I had our rifles ready, aimed at the spots where we knew our targets would appear. We had decided to let them disperse in the exercise yard before starting to fire. We did not want to hit any of the guards.

As time passed I felt more and more tense. Smoking did not help. But I told myself that I had to be calm, that all this planning and waiting must not be wasted by my nerves. And after ten minutes of the inner "shakes" I did manage to get hold of myself. Reuben looked perfectly composed, though later he told me that he also had butterflies in his stomach.

Then Simon arrived. He was panting and perspiring, quite

unlike his usual well-groomed and assured self. He said, "It's all off, boys. I was so worried I wouldn't get here in time."

"Off?" Both Reuben and I sounded incredulous. "What do you mean?"

"There were three messages at the office when I got there. Janek was almost out of his mind with worry. He thought we might do it first and only pick up the tickets afterwards."

"What messages?" I asked. "Who sent them?"

"Our security service in Tel Aviv. Janek reported to Aaron, and Aaron reported to his superiors. They don't want us to do it. Not for the time being."

Reuben began to swear. He could swear very well in three languages—Polish, German, and Hebrew. I said nothing, but I felt empty and cheated.

"But why? Why?"

Simon shrugged. "I don't know. Something about negotiation with Germany on repatriations that may start before very long."

"Sure," I said bitterly, "maybe if they pay enough money all the Nazi murderers in prison will be released and all the murders will be forgiven."

"Now, Emil," Simon said, "you know that's not true. Besides, this doesn't mean we have to give up our work. Janek has a suggestion. Let's go back and talk to him."

We wrapped our precious rifles in sacking, which we put in a sleeping-bag. Then we buried them in a spot that was easily accessible. They must still be there, under the foundations of the modern studio which Arthur B built on the site of the old, half-demolished tannery.

43

Janek's idea wasn't so bad, though in our frustrated and cantankerous mood anything would have appealed to us that promised action. The sum-total of our achievements was the Eichmann photograph, and even that was mostly David's doing—we only supplied the escort.

Janek suggested that we should go to Munich. The Bavarian capital was the real birthplace of the Nazi movement, he said; it was still solidly reactionary and unrepentant and many of

170

the ex-Nazis had taken refuge in and around it. It was in the American zone of Germany, and, with the Cold War getting colder every minute the SS and Gestapo men who had gone underground felt reasonably safe. Their thinking was simple enough: they had fought the Communist menace and therefore had been on the right side. That in the process they had murdered millions of non-Communists did not make any difference according to their reasoning. They deserved to be appreciated and praised—or at the very least to be left alone.

We were given the names of three members of the organization which Aaron headed in Vienna. They were Jews who had spent the war in Germany, or at least had lived in the defeated country since the end of the war. All three spoke German perfectly, all three were experts in the hunter's game. Janek promised that we would get from them a list of "candidates", and that this time there would be no interference from anyone.

We arrived in Munich on March 9th. We stayed there until the end of April. And during these seven weeks we killed sixteen people.

44

Let me call the three men who met us in the Bavarian capital Abe, Berak, and Ceslaw. They had been at their job for much longer than we had; they were true professionals. They were in no way our superiors, for we three were a self-contained, independent unit, guerrillas or freebooters, if you like. We had no intention of making this our life's work, but all three of us felt the burning need to cleanse ourselves of hate and grief by doing what we had to do.

Abe and his friends had lists—lists of a number of Germans who had served in the Gestapo and the SS and who were directly responsible for the massacres, the tortures, the executioners' work that all but exterminated our people. They were people who had gone scot-free, whom nobody had called to account, who had, by various means, escaped the process of denazification. It was not difficult to buy or blackmail witnesses into perjury, to forge documents, and to prepare alibis. Certainly the West German Government wasn't going to take any action—not at that time. All through the years that followed

171

there were renewed scandals when it turned out that this or that high-ranking official, politician, judge, military commander, had a Nazi past. Those who could covered up for one another. Not everybody could or wanted to escape, though the various underground organizations were still busy helping the most heavily compromised war criminals to reach the safety of South America or Egypt.

But we had to be careful and we had to make doubly sure. There had been thousands of SS men (though not very many Gestapo) who had not taken part in the mass murder of Jews, whose jobs in that vast organization were purely administrative or far removed from the "final solution". They may have committed other crimes in the West or the East, they may have robbed or bullied their way to a comfortable fortune, but they were not our concern. What we wanted was detailed and incontrovertible information about those whom we intended to punish.

Scores of our people who had been living in Germany since the end of the war, or even before it, had occupied themselves entirely with the gathering of this information. The Nazis believed that they had killed all witnesses. In the death camps the Jewish *Sonderkommandos*, the detachments who buried or cremated the dead, who removed the gold teeth and carefully sorted out the pitiful loot which they provided, were periodically sent to the gas-chambers or shot. But there were survivors. By some miracle, by sheer luck, or by some extraordinary courage there were enough of those who remained alive to provide the necessary material. When this or that SS man was said to have been active in the ghetto of Byalistok or Wilno our people did not rest until they found survivors. By showing photographs or, quite often, bringing these witnesses to places where they could see the ex-Nazis still at large they obtained all the necessary material. Nor was it just handled individually, unsystematically. There were two centres where all this material was collected and carefully checked—one in Vienna, another in Munich. All this took time, but neither we nor the organization wanted to act without being absolutely sure that we were carrying out acts of real justice.

The final list which we received after we had been about a week in Munich consisted of twenty names. We executed all but four, as these had either moved or, in the case of one, died of natural causes in the meantime.

45

Everything was planned carefully and meticulously. We did not stay at the same boarding-house or in the same furnished rooms. Each of us moved every three or four days. It was only once that the police came to the place where I had lived and asked whether any foreigners were still residing there; they were told that I had already left. We did not meet in cafés or restaurants, but in the streets or squares, discussing our tasks while we were window-shopping, pretending to be waiting for a tram, or queuing up outside a theatre or concert-hall. It was still pretty cold and, especially in the evening, there weren't too many people around. We had a number of addresses and always communicated by telephone or messenger. No-one was called or visited more than once at the same address by any of us. We never met publicly, the three of us, but stayed apart and kept in touch only through go-betweens, except when we were actually carrying out one of our "expeditions".

For these we used cars which we either stole or hired under an assumed name—that is, Abe or one of his two friends did, lest a foreign accent should be remembered. And the cars were either promptly returned to the hire firm or, if stolen, abandoned immediately after we had finished with them.

Of the sixteen executions I took part in seven, Reuben in ten, and Simon in six. There were others after we left and there had been a few before we arrived, but those did not concern us.

Our method was simple enough. Abe, or Berak, or Ceslaw would telephone the man who was next on our list. Naturally, by then we had studied his habits, his way of life, we knew when he was likely to be at home, which cafés or beer-gardens he frequented, how many people there were in his family, how he dressed, whether he was in good physical condition or not. The telephone-call was designed to utilize all this information. It was an invitation to some place which he had visited before, or the offer of some business deal; it was always different and perfectly adjusted to each man's character and business interests. They all felt quite safe; few of them were in touch with each other, just because they obviously wanted to break with their past, to bury it as deep as possible. I think their sense of security came from the profound contempt they had always felt for their victims, whether Jews, Slavs, gipsies, or Latins, for they were, after all, the *Herrenvolk* and the fact of the defeat did not change that conviction, at least not for those men who had been members of the élite.

When they answered the phone-call we were waiting for them downstairs, either in the lobby of their houses or apartments or in the street. Sometimes one of us rented a room right opposite, so that we could watch them for some length of time. But it was easy, at least in those cases in which I took part. We bundled them in the car and gagged them. Then we told them. We did not abuse them or curse them; we were long past that. We told them exactly who we were, so that they should have no illusions in their last few minutes of life; and we told them about the crimes, where they had committed them, what suffering they had caused, and how many lives they had taken.

Sometimes we poured brandy or vodka down their throats and then knocked them out. We took great care to make every execution look like an accident. When we had made them swallow half a bottle of spirits we took them to the Neckar or some other smaller river and held them under the water until they drowned. Then we left them there. Once or twice we ran them down with the car, making sure they were dead. And on one occasion in which I participated we followed our man when he went out shooting. There were three of them, but we had no quarrel with two of the three. We followed them, and when they became separated we shot *our* quarry. We shot him, after we had pinioned his arms behind, from so close that it looked as if he had accidentally shot himself, powder-burns and all. It was not that we were worried about being caught, though that was not our intention; we knew that others would take up our work when we had finished and we did not want to arouse suspicion. As a matter of fact, it was only once that some people rushed after us when we had run over one of our war criminals, but we got away and abandoned our car. Anyhow, we never used a car that could be traced to us. There was some mention in the papers of a mysterious car and they did report "fatal accidents", but there was no linking them to war crimes, to the fact that the victims had all been in the SS or the Gestapo. In any case, by the time these reports began to appear we were no longer in Munich.

174

One by one the names on our list were crossed off. I could recall them if I wanted, but I have closed the door upon those memories, and it is better that it stay shut. During those seven weeks we slept little, ate only to keep going, and did not waste time on thinking about what we were doing and why. It was a mission we had to carry out; working against time, we were only anxious to have it done. I can say only one thing: among those in whose liquidation I took part was the SS officer who had ordered the mass execution in Bukovinka forest.

46

I took a plane to Rome and changed to another to get to Tel Aviv. Reuben went to Vienna. Simon made his way to Paris, then to Brussels, and arrived in Israel a few weeks after I did.

I had been away less than six months, but it seemed a very long time. Israel was now a fully established, independent country: we had even had our first budget, and, like any large and older country, there was a deficit. There seemed no prospect of any peace negotiations, but, apart from an occasional Arab raid, a little shelling, and some sneak attacks, there was peace. And there was work to do—so much work!

Less than a year later I met Hanka, who had come to Israel from Switzerland, where she had worked as a laboratory assistant. I fell in love with her at first sight. Three months after our first meeting we were married. Of course, the time came when I had to go to war—in 1956 and again in 1967—but both times it was no longer fighting with bare hands, against impossible odds, for our very lives. And now, as I am coming to the end of my story, there is even a glimmer of hope that we and the Arabs will be able to cast off the old griefs and grievances, the many centuries of senseless hate, and start living together. It will not be easy and there may be many setbacks and arguments, but we can wait, we can sweat it out. It can never be as bad as it was in the Polish forest, the Hungarian prison. We are a nation and we will always have the arms to defend ourselves if the tragic need arises.

Until that night when I took Roni to the seashore I had not told my full story to anyone, not even to Hanka. I had settled accounts with the world and myself. I am not a man much given to introspection and self-analysis. I did what I had to and I would do it again if the necessity arose, though I hope it will never happen again.

I know that there will be people who will judge me harshly. To them I can only say that a corpse cannot turn the other cheek, and that if vengeance is the Lord's that is scant consolation to those rotting in the mass graves. Gandhi was a great man, but if he had been alive he could not have stopped the Chinese tanks or the Pakistani planes. Non-violence is a beautiful idea as long as there are no man-eating tigers, two- or four-legged, at large.

Think of all that was destroyed and erased during the years of the holocaust! How many symphonies, how many great paintings, how many beautiful poems, have been smothered in the minds of the millions who died in the gas-chambers and the forests! How many great discoveries which would have benefited the whole world have died with them! Their loss is not only a loss to the Jewish race, but to all mankind. And if our fight saved a single one for the future—the father of a new Einstein, the mother of a new Chagall—was it not worth it?

I do not know, and I am not asking for judgment, acquittal, or sympathy. I was turned into a killer because others killed. I have put aside my gun, and I never want to take it up again. But if the call came once more I would still stand up and fight.